Diagnosis
and Detection

Diagnosis and Detection

The Medical Iconography of Sherlock Holmes

Pasquale Accardo, M.D.

Rutherford • Madison • Teaneck
Fairleigh Dickinson University Press
London and Toronto: Associated University Presses

© 1987 by Associated University Presses, Inc.

Associated University Presses
440 Forsgate Drive
Cranbury, NJ 08512

Associated University Presses
25 Sicilian Avenue
London WC1A 2QH, England

Associated University Presses
2133 Royal Windsor Drive
Unit 1
Mississauga, Ontario
Canada L5J 1K5

The paper used in this publication meets the requirements of the American National Standard for Permanence of Paper for Printed Library Materials Z39.48-1984.

Library of Congress Cataloging-in-Publication Data

Accardo, Pasquale J.
   Diagnosis and detection.

  Bibliography: p.
  Includes index.
  1. Doyle, Arthur Conan, Sir, 1859–1930—Knowledge—Medicine. 2. Doyle, Arthur Conan, Sir, 1859–1930—Characters—Sherlock Holmes. 3. Medicine in literature.
4. Holmes, Sherlock (Fictitious character)
5. Detective and mystery stories—History and criticism.   I. Title.
PR4624.A22   1987   823'.8   86-45057
ISBN 0-8386-3292-0 (alk. paper)

Printed in the United States of America

*To my parents
who on a Christmas morning many years ago
first introduced me to
the pleasures of these unique adventures*

The mission of thought is to construct archetypes; I mean, to point out from among the infinite figures that reality presents those in which, because of their greater purity, that reality becomes clearer.

—Ortega y Gassett

Contents

Acknowledgments		9
1	Introduction: A Case of Identifiers	13
2	The Mythic Structure of the Sherlock Holmes Canon: Epic, Saga, and Medieval Romance	17
3	The Medical Model	22
4	Literary Archetypes	42
5	The General Theory of Detection: Sense and Non-Sense in Science	70
6	The Special Theory of Detection: The Semiology of Sherlock Holmes	84
7	The Book of Watson: An Uncertain Friendship	97
8	Conclusion: The Unified Field Theory of Detection	106
Appendix: Quantitative Stylistic Analysis of the Sixty Sherlock Holmes Stories and Selected Pastiches		112
Notes		125
Bibliography		134
Index		137

Acknowledgments

Grateful acknowledgment is made to the following:

A. S. Barnes and Company, Inc., for permission to quote from Samuel Tenenbaum, *The Wise Men of Chelm*.

Columbia University Press, for permission to quote from James H. Austin, *Chase, Chance and Creativity*.

Dodd, Mead and Company, Inc., and A. P. Watt, Ltd., for permission to quote from G. K. Chesterton, *The Father Brown Omnibus*.

Gambit, Inc., for permission to quote from Giorgio de Santillana and Hertha von Dechend, *Hamlet's Mill*.

Harcourt, Brace and World and Faber and Faber, Ltd., for permission to quote from T. S. Eliot, *The Complete Poems and Plays 1909–1950*.

Holly Stevens and Alfred A. Knopf, for permission to quote from Wallace Stevens, *The Palm at the End of the Mind*.

Jeanne Young and Susan Harding demonstrated exceptional deductive skills in their decoding of the original handwritten manuscript.

Diagnosis
and Detection

1
Introduction: A Case of Identifiers

> Your speech is simple, my Master, but not theirs who talk of you
> —Tagore

> When the text is clear do not make it obscure by thy commentary
> —Jacopone da Todi

> Fools make the text, and witty men the commentaries
> —Galieni

Medical education and a detective story frequently begin with the same object—a dead body. But while the murder mystery closes with the guilty party discovered and all the plot threads unraveled, it is rare for the first-year anatomy student to be able to identify the cause of death for his or her cadaver. Indeed, this state of ignorance and uncertainty, of questions without final answers, remains quite characteristic of the practice of medicine despite an intensive public-relations campaign to invest the physician with the cloak of certitude more correctly worn by the laboratory sciences that serve as the handmaidens to medicine. Because science deals only with non-unique events, there can be no science of the individual. The general truths of science may be applied to individual phenomena with greater or lesser degrees of accuracy. The success of such applications will depend on principles belonging not to a science but to an art of medicine/detection. William Osler suggested that half the material being taught in medical schools was false but that no one knew which half. Despite the increasing emphasis on the scientific content of medical education, his estimate is probably still true today.

Arthur Conan Doyle was a writer of mediocre talent who had the innocence and luck to combine certain mythic elements to produce a viable modern hero. In the field of medicine he was much less than mediocre, and literature's gain probably saved many lives. The present exploration of Doyle's sources, medical and literary, is in no way meant to reduce Sherlock Holmes to a variation on some other character, real or imaginary. Holmes, neither the first nor the last of his kind, remains the archetype. Despite numerous ancestors and progeny, the problem of his continued preeminent status has never been adequately addressed.

The pseudoscholarship prevalent in the literature of Sherlock Holmes testifies indirectly and obscurely to the existential vitality of the characters and events narrated in the original stories. In the annals of popular literature, the "writings upon the writings" reflect a phenomenon perversely unique for two reasons: first, they contribute little or nothing to explain the immense popularity of the characters whether in the original Doyle stories or in their countless plagiarisms, pastiches, parodies, and other reincarnations. Second, they accept their basic principles of critical analysis from the original tales themselves and apply Holmes's rules for detection to unsolved and artifactual pseudoproblems inherent in the narrative.

The present essay deviates from this pattern in several ways. First, it is concerned with the character(s) Holmes/Watson, where (t)he(y) come(s) from, and what mythic echoes reverberate throughout the tales to contribute to their status as popular classics. Second, it finds Sherlock Holmes's explanation of his own powers of deduction to be superficial and misleading as practical methodology and downright false as scientific theory. Too much credibility has been assigned to Holmes's account of what he did (his endlessly requoted maxims on facts, observation, and deduction), whereas too little attention has been paid to what he actually did.

A mystery narrative first of all tells a story. Information is provided by the plot events—cardinal functions (nuclei) and catalyzers—and indices proper describe the characters, their feelings, and the atmosphere of the story. Finally, informants locate the narrative in a particular era, time and place. At a second level (connoted rather than denoted) the detective story has many symbolic meanings that are fairly obvious (e.g., good versus evil). But there is a third level of significance (the noncoded iconic message) that is easily overlooked. Barthes refers to this elusive and fleeting supplement as the obtuse meaning and relates it to the pun, buffoonery, and the carnival. This third "message without a code" is simultaneously unintentional, de-

Table 1
Levels of Meaning in Narrative[1]

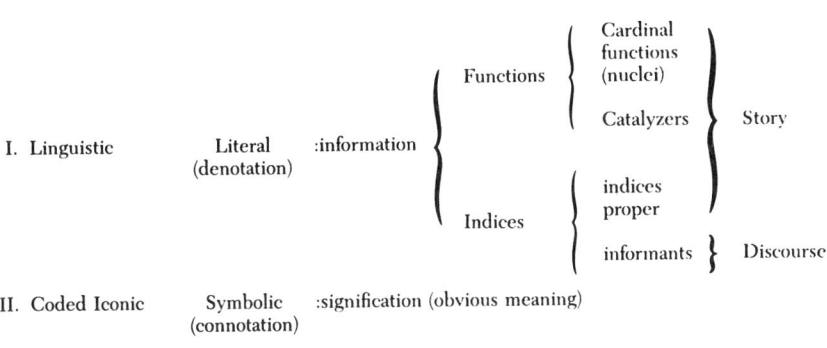

risory, and indifferent to the obvious meaning, subverting and even contradicting the first two levels of meaning (see table 1).

The irony of extant Sherlockian scholarship is that it has focused almost exclusively on the first level of meaning, especially informants (boring minutiae Victorianae), the least revealing component of the narrative structure. Further, while these informants have been tortured to surrender conclusions both inconsequential and questionable, their relevance to the structure of discourse has been almost totally ignored. Needless to say, such detailed textual analyses yield results that quite simply violate the canons of elementary psychology and outrage common sense. These absurdities are all perpetrated in deference to a rigorous application of Holmes's own stated method. What is overlooked is the fact that Holmes lied.

By restricting the search for meaning to level I (with an occasional reference to level II), the contributions of that third level (revolutionary and subversive to the more superficial and obvious interpretations) to an understanding of the genius of the work are ignored. The present investigation seeks to explore this third meaning by tracking the known medical and literary models for the classic deductive sequences that open most of the Sherlock Holmes stories. Jungian analysis of those "vague memories in our souls of those misty centuries when the world was in its childhood" (*A Study of Scarlet*) will be kept to a minimum; texts will be allowed to speak for themselves.

With regard to the ontological argument, the present work is neutral: the existence of Sherlock Holmes is a hypothesis unnecessary to the argument of this book. Nevertheless, there should not be interpreted the slightest hint of any intent to debunk or demythologize; on the usual spectrum of Sherlockian criticism, this is a fundamentalist (albeit in a radical sense) work. How the practicing physician thinks (or fails to) and (mis)diagnoses will remain the practical psychological and epistemological touchstone for these researches.

Finally, the author must confess to an aversion for detective fiction. A prolonged involvement in medical education has familiarized him with the bravura and boasting of a troubled health delivery system, its illusions and delusions, its predilection for pretense and mystification. Interests in the Middle Ages, the Napoleonic period, and the Victorian era round out his limited qualifications to enter the chaotic arena of Holmesian scholarship. Unrepentently unclubable, he belongs to no Holmesian societies.

Footnotes for "ritual adornment and terror" have been kept to a minimum, and direct quotations from the Canon have been avoided whenever possible as a matter of principle. These research notes are addressed *neque indoctissimis neque doctissimis* but to that dear and gentle reader who enjoys the tales and the pleasure of the hunt.

2
The Mythic Structure of the Sherlock Holmes Canon: Epic, Saga, and Medieval Romance

> One man opposing a society
> If properly misunderstood becomes a myth
> —Wallace Stevens

> And Holmes, whose name shall live in epic song
> While music numbers, or while verse has feet
> —Dryden, *Annus Mirabilis*

> He is one of the last incarnations of chivalry in the literature of the English language.
> —Pierre Nordon

> For we move in the footsteps of others, and all life is but the pouring of the present into the forms of myth.
> —Thomas Mann, *Joseph in Egypt*

The epic that epitomizes any given age is written when that age is nearing its end, when its carefully realized ethos is seriously threatened by decay and conflict from within:

> In these ages of misfortune
> When the race is near its ending.[2]

The old order is under increasing pressure from new disruptive forces. Robert Lifton notes that one reaction to a perceived threat of chaos is a nostalgic vision of a golden age with exact boundaries, an age in which men allegedly knew exactly where they stood.[3] Homer, Virgil, Dante, Milton, and Goethe all sing of such mythical pasts, but neither these poets nor their first readers were actually aware that their subject matter was the past, and instead, many critics praised their modernity.

This characteristic of epic poetry aptly describes one of the striking features of Doyle's Sherlock Holmes stories: they tell of a bygone heroic age. Although some modern commentators read into these detective tales a romanticization of Victorian conservativism, neither Doyle nor his first readers perceived any trace of nostalgia in the very up-to-date Holmes. The singular characteristic of the stories is the manner in which they combine a purported scientific modernity with a presumed set of values that had already died at the center at the time Doyle wrote. The golden age of Victoria Regina with its vicious underworld, crass commercialism, sexual perversion, and child prostitution encountered in Sherlock Holmes an adversarial hero, a countercultural phenomenon that numerous critics persist in misinterpreting as proestablishment.

While Doyle's work certainly does not fit the mold for literary or romantic epics, it does have much in common with the oral epics that idealize the heroic spirit: "The heroic world holds nothing so important as the prowess and fame of the individual hero. The single man, Achilles or Beowulf or Roland, surpasses others in strength and courage. His chief, almost his only aim is to win honour and renown through his achievements and to be remembered for them after his death . . . In his more than human strength he seems to be cut off from the intercourse of common men and consorts with a few companions only less noble than himself. He lacks allegiance, except in a modified sense, to suzerain or cause. What matters is his prowess. Even morality hardly concerns him; for he lives in a world where what counts is not morality but honour."[4] This anarchic oral tradition exhibits constantly repeated epithets and lines, a spirit of improvisation, and an apparent carelessness about details with a concentrated focus on general effect—all traits that modern Sherlockian critics continually try to explain away as reflections of Watsonian deficiencies.

A careful comparison of the character of Sherlock Holmes with more primitive epic heroes would easily document that Holmes was not some degenerate offshoot but rather that pristine antisocial hero sprung full grown from Doyle's brow. Like Holmes, the epic hero usually appears mature upon the scene in medias res;[5] in contrast, the Grail romances often detail the ancestry, birth, youth, appareling, education, and early exploits of the hero. But from the gest romances

Doyle did take their sense of exoticism and mystery, their almost total exclusion of woman, and a structure of loosely linked episodic adventures with only fragmentary backgrounds. Like King Arthur and Gargantua,[6] his main character tried to maintain a singular aloofness, and his tales were authenticated as originating from documented sources. (This last aspect is probably the only one that has been creatively handled by numerous Doyle imitators. But Watson's tin dispatch box was either a steamer trunk or he etched his notes on microdots.) There are even occasional overseas voyages (Celtic *imrama*, or journey literature). Finally, Doyle puts a totally new interpretation on the most striking of romance customs—the holding of consultations to interpret dreams: through his exposition of symbols, the hermit seer or holy man helps a character decide on a direction in life. Frequently, the noncriminal irregularities that are brought to Holmes's attention fill his clients with the same sense of foreboding as a troublesome dream. Life cannot continue in its assumed course until these upsetting events have been rendered intelligible, and the oldest and most durable form of intelligibility is the myth.

The past that is evoked in the Sherlock Holmes stories is not that of Victorian England but echoes of an older mythic time. In this primordial timelessness there exist patterns of action that are eternal and that men episodically imitate in order to participate in true being. These mythic patterns allow many variations and so exhibit recurrence, repetition, rebirth, reincarnation, resurrection, and eternal recurrence. The repertoire of possible meanings is limited, and the limited treasure of significant occurrences is held sacred. Memories and intuitions of mythic time can be attached to historic personages, but history is not at the root of myth. Indeed, the myth seems to precede the historical event to which it becomes attached.

In his own lifetime, chroniclers and troubadours began to apply to King Richard I of England (1157–99) ancient myths and Arthurian legends to the extent that careful literary analysis would later be needed to distinguish fact from fiction.[7] A demon mother, a magical sword (Excalibur/Balmung/Vaiduryakanti/Joyeuse/Durendal), angelic visitations, and the nun's eyes were some of the folk legends that became attached to Richard Coeur de Lion's biography. A criminological myth associated with Richard was the tale that the nose of Henry's corpse bled when Richard approached his father's bier. The reopening of the wounds of a murdered man was believed to identify his killer, but in this case the tale was probably meant to indicate that Richard's long and violent quarreling with his father had contributed to the latter's demise. The magical ability of blood to identify a murderer would be taken over and appropriately transformed by the new scientific mythos, and Sherlock Holmes would make his own contribution to this deep-rooted dream of forensic pathology. The dean of all twentieth-century charlatans, Dr. Albert Abrams, would claim that "a drop of blood represents the entire individual and suffices for diagnosis."[8]

The freedom of myth from historic time is well reflected in the historical fact of Richard's famous imprisonment for ransom by Leopold, duke of Austria (Modred), being translated in time from after to before the First Crusade. This revised temporal sequence allowed a greater glorification of Richard's exploits in the Holy Land. Such a displacement has not yet been hypothesized to explain the puzzling occurrence of the death of Sherlock Holmes at the hands of Professor Moriarity in the middle of the saga because critics have insisted on locating these events in historic time. In mythic time, Holmes could have both really died at the Reichenbach Falls *and* later retired to beekeeping in Sussex.

The Napoleonic myth offers a more contemporary example of the way in which myth confuses rational categories. Napoleon dominated the opening of the nineteenth century as much by an appeal to the imagination as by an appeal to arms. Few historical characters have so carefully cultivated romanticism, have so consciously authored their own dramatic parts for the historical stage. Bonaparte combined elements of the classic (Paoli: "You come from the age of Plutarch") and the romantic ("What a novel my life has been") to produce what Ferrero described as "a *chanson de geste* in prose, composed for a bourgeois era."[9] In the words of Albert Guérard: "The *career* of Napoleon, viewed from the standpoint of the professional dramatist, is a masterpiece of stagecraft; the *character* of Napoleon, if it were the creation of a fiction writer, would be pronounced shallow and uninteresting."[10] Lie, bluff, skillful public relations, the myth of the invincibility of the Grand Armée was first broken in the guerrilla fighting in Spain, reduced to frozen immobility in the icy wastes of Russia, and finally buried at Waterloo. In contrast, the myth of the return never quite died: the return from Italy, from Egypt, from central Europe, from Russia, from Elba . . . from St. Helena.

Distinct from the usual Napoleonic polemics, such deliberate attempts at creating a heroic figure of exaggerated proportions contributed to the possibility of an Anglican archbishop proving two years before Napoleon's death that no such historic personage ever existed.[11] Utilizing a different kind of skepticism, a French ecclesiastic amassed arguments that reduced Napoleon to a solar myth (e.g., Napoleon = Né-Apoleón = Apollo; Napoleon's mother was Letitia, Apollo's was Leto, and both had three sisters; the French marshals were given a zodiacal interpretation, and Napoleon's star was noted to rise in the east and set in the west).[12] Needless to say, both clerics employed these modes of critical analysis as examples of reductio ad absurdum.

Science, according to Karl Popper, is distinct from the older myths only in being accompanied by a second-order tradition—the critical discussion of the myth. The literature of Sherlock Holmes has developed its own critical apparatus but has not succeeded in identifying the central myth underlying Doyle's series of detective tales. From the French Revolution, Napoleon inherited the myth of equality, which he spread over Europe. The rewarding of ability rather than privilege was very slow in coming to England. When the ability was scientific knowledge and when privilege cloaked bureaucratic incompetence, the radical countercultural position of Sherlock Holmes becomes obvious. The central myth of the Holmes saga is that knowledge, especially scientific knowledge, can be made to serve human ends. While this might seem a truism to the Victorian and modern ages, its essential falsity had already been documented by the blight of the Industrial Revolution and the nightmarish science fiction futures described by H. G. Wells.[13] Sherlock Holmes was living proof that there was still room to hope that science could be humanized. That the successful use of a medical model to reinforce this otherwise paradoxical conception was not accidental is the subject of the next chapter.[14]

3
The Medical Model

When a doctor goes wrong he is the first of criminals.
—Doyle

He played his part without knowledge of his predecessors and successors in it, as though he were its first and only actor—for each of us must consider himself that in every part he plays, as though he had made it all up himself, yet with a sureness and dignity which comes to him, when he plays it, so to speak, in daylight for the first time, not from his supposed invention of the role, but on the contrary from the well-grounded consciousness that he is once more presenting something legitimate and traditional, and must perform it, however repellent, to the best of his ability according to the pattern.
—Thomas Mann, *Joseph in Egypt*

ARTHUR CONAN DOYLE

You are yourself Sherlock Holmes!
—Joseph Bell to Arthur C. Doyle

Holmes was to a large extent Conan Doyle himself.
—Adrian Conan Doyle

That untidy boy with his strange power of observation.
—Marquis of Villavieja on his classmate A. C. Doyle

What is once well done is done forever.
—Thoreau

Anybody, almost, can make a beginning: the difficulty is to make an end—to do what cannot be bettered.
—*Shaw on Music*

The Medical Model

Arthur Conan Doyle was a Scottish physician-writer born in 1859. His early schooling was at the hands of the Jesuits of Stonyhurst. He then studied medicine at the University of Edinburgh under such brilliant clinicians as Dr. Joseph Bell and took his Bachelor of Medicine and Master of Surgery in 1881 and his M.D. degree in 1885. He worked as a ship's doctor on Arctic whalers, voyaged to the West African coast, went into medical partnership with a psychopathic quack, and came close to starving in a solo practice. In 1891 he spent several months in Vienna in a futile attempt to subspecialize in ophthalmology, joined the Ophthalmological Society of the United Kingdom, opened an oculist's office close to prestigious Harley Street, and then, to the salvation of many a patient, gave up the practice of medicine to pursue a full-time literary career.[15]

Although he achieved phenomenal success as a writer, especially as the creator of Sherlock Holmes, Doyle came to regard his fictional detective as some kind of Frankenstein monster who detracted from the public's appreciation of his true literary worth: "All things find their level, but I believe that if I had never touched Holmes, who tended to obscure my higher work, my position in literature would at the present moment be a more commanding one."[16]

Doyle's growing distaste for the popularity of his detective cannot be attributed merely to the fact that this hero returned (even from the grave) in more than sixty sequels; all his better characters did the same. The Gascon adventurer Etienne Gerard *(l'audace, et encore de l'audace, et toujours de l'audace)* brought Napoleonic France alive in the Brigadier Gerard series;[17] Professor George Edward Challanger personified muscular Victorian scientism in several science fiction classics, and Sir Nigel Loring's gesta were recorded in the tediously accurate historical novels that Doyle considered his highest literary achievement—*The White Company* and *Sir Nigel*—if only Holmes hadn't interfered. If Holmes, Gerard, Challanger, and Sir Nigel represented different aspects of Doyle's personality, how could one of them overwhelm his creator? How could the part be greater than the whole?

Doyle disclaimed any significant contribution from earlier English fictional detectives to his portrayal of Holmes, and certainly the traces of William Godwin's Caleb Williams, Charles Dickens's Inspector Bucket, and Wilkie Collins' Sergeant Cuff are slight. It somehow seemed more fitting for Holmes to have real-life medical-scientific prototypes rather than literary ones. The bookish Doyle could not bring himself to accept Huxley's dictum that the proper study of mankind is books. While Dr. Oliver Wendell Holmes provided a name with both literary and scientific associations, the main inspiration that Doyle acknowledged was his old medical school teacher, Dr. Joseph Bell.

The diagnostic skill and personality traits of Sir William Arbuthnot Lane (1856–1943) made him another medical model for Holmes. An active and innovative professional, Lane was senior surgeon at both Guys Hospital and the Hospital for Sick Children, Great Ormond Street. This address perhaps inspired the name of Ormond Sacker, who was the narrator in Conan Doyle's manuscript, *A Tangled Skein*. (When published in 1887, the narrator's name and the title of the novel were changed to John H. Watson and *A Study in Scarlet*, respectively.) Lane was also rumored to be the original Doctor Cutler Walpole in Shaw's *Doctor's Dilemma*. Unfortunately, "Lane's disease" was a very unscientific amalgamation of the older myth of Glénard's disease (visceroptosis) with the newer myth of autointoxication (self-poisoning) and resulted in many unfortunate patients being subjected to unnecessary ileosigmoidostomies and colectomies. Dr. Lane was one of the prophets of the twentieth-century religion of (bowel) regularity.[18]

Doyle is supposed to have left numerous clues to his own (partially) unconscious identification with his most famous creation. Both Sherlock Holmes and Arthur Conan Doyle had Irish names and were descended from a family of squires with prominent artists (Antoine, Claude, Carle, and Horace Vernet/John Doyle) and French blood. Both men had gray eyes, one brother, a friend named Dr. J. Watson, a secondary reputation for nonfictional writing (monographs on detective and other subjects/military propaganda and spiritualist tracts), an encyclopedic if often superficial range of interests (highlighted by an almost morbid curiosity in murder and mayhem), and a passion for dressing gowns and pipe tobacco stored in slippers. Both were sportsmen (boxing and fencing), were chivalrous to a fault, were manic depressive, were monist (materialist/spiritualist), had a horror of destroying documents (and, therefore, large cumbrous files), perused the popular press, irritatingly played a musical instrument (violin/brass horn), and (almost, in Doyle's case) declined a knighthood.

According to his son Adrian, Doyle had the same power of keen observation that characterized Holmes: a glance at clothes and physical habitus enabled him to (accurately?) deduce a stranger's life history. Dostoyevsky's *Diary of a Writer* (1873) records his preoccupation with closely observing strangers, guessing at who they were, how they lived, what kind of work they did, what presently interested them, and then inventing episodes in their lives to coincide with his fabricated portraits.[19] These were exercises in creative imagination rather than logical deduction but they certainly required the latter.

Several of the real-life criminal cases in which Doyle was successfully engaged testify to his concern for the victims of bureaucratic injustice. But they also bear witness to the wide gulf separating the two detectives: the most striking quality of Doyle's solutions to the cases of horse mutilation (George Edalji) and murder (Oscar Slater) is their total lack of adventure, insight, and anything approaching brilliant deduction. They represent instead shining examples of plodding investigation, problems that any rural constable of middling intelligence could have solved if he had set his mind to it. The level of interest of the cases is such that Holmes would have declined to undertake them even when afflicted with the severest boredom. Doyle's own detective work is the strongest proof that he was not Sherlock Holmes.

Doyle's concept of a great author was someone in complete conscious control of his characters; he once referred to Holmes and Watson as "my puppets." He retreated like Hemingway into the assumption that public praise was always misdirected to the worst aspects of one's work. "Literature" could not be clumsily and hastily written, with bourgeois themes, and for crass, financial motives—except, of course, by Balzac, Cervantes, Dostoyevsky, Dickens, Poe, Shakespeare, and a host of other hacks. If Holmes's oversimplification of scientific method can appropriately be described as "high school," so can Doyle's misconception of great literature. It was not that the public misunderstood which were Doyle's more important works; they understood better than he did, because they actively participated in the immortalization of his characters. As he had rejected the Catholicism of his childhood, so he balked at the promised literary immortality of a writer of detective fiction. He chose, instead, to follow in the footsteps of the chemist, William Crookes, and the codiscoverer of evolution, Alfred Russel Wallace, and was converted to spiritualism. To a Catholic (capital and/or lower case "c") sensibility the popularity of Holmes was easily intelligible; to the more pompous and smug spiritualist aesthetic, it could represent only a blasphemous parody of an all too serious truth.

The remaining details of Doyle's life are, in Martin Gardner's phrase, irrelevant to the understanding of Sherlock Holmes.[20]

A TINTINNABULARY BELL

"And yet you say he is not a medical student?"
—A. C. Doyle

> Doctors are trained by other doctors. Each physician, then, is not only himself but is made up of other men, and each teacher becomes a part of his students.
> —Eric Cassell, *The Healer's Art*

> *Ars medica tota in observationibus*
> —Osler

> Spot diagnosis you should hate
> Until you are a surgeon great.
> —Zeta

Joseph Bell was professor of surgery at the University of Edinburgh when Arthur Doyle lackadaisically matriculated there. Bell was an imposing and memorable character both as a physician and as a teacher. "Thin, wiry, dark with a high nosed acute face, penetrating grey eyes, angular shoulders, and a jerky way of walking"—Doyle would remember "his sharp piercing eyes, eagle nose, and striking features"[21] years later when the young author consciously set about to add a new dimension to the detective genre: "I thought of my old teacher, Joe Bell, of his eagle face, of his curious way, of his eerie trick of spotting details. If he were a detective, he would surely reduce this fascinating, but unorganized, business into something nearer to an exact science. It was surely possible in real life, so why should I not make it plausible in fiction. It is all very well to say that a man is clever, but the reader wants to see examples of it . . . such examples as Bell gave us every day in the wards."[22]

Bell was "a very skillful surgeon, but his strong point was diagnosis, not only of disease, but of occupation and character"; before examining patients, "he would tell them their symptoms, and even the details of their past life, and would hardly ever make a mistake."[23] On the dull side of normal, like Watson, the impressionable Doyle was easily awed by Bell's parlor tricks: he "would tell us where all the other passengers in the carriage were from, where they were going, and something of their occupation and habits. All this without having spoken to them. When he verified his observations, we thought him a magician."[24] Bell sensed that the athletic "60% for effort" medical student would make a perfect foil and appointed Doyle his out-patient clerk: "I had ample chance of studying his methods and in noticing that he often learned more of the patient by a few quick glances than I had done by my questions."[25]

As a teacher, Bell stressed the careful observation of details: "I always impressed over and over again upon my students the vast importance of little distinctions, the endless significance of the trifles. . . . Eyes and ears which can see and hear, memory to record at once . . . precise and intelligent recognition and appreciation of minor differences as the essential factor in all successful medical diagnosis." He was aided a great deal in his diagnostic coups by the fact that Victorian society was heavily stratified; clothes, body habitus, and other markings could quickly locate individuals in their place in the hierarchy: "Nearly every handicraft writes its sign-manual on the hands. The scars of the miner differ from those of the quarryman. The carpenter's callosities are not those of the mason. . . . The soldier and sailor differ in gait. Accent helps you to district and, to an educated ear, almost to county."[26] (Shades of Professor Henry Higgins!)

This skill in deducing occupation and life history from trifling details had its more famous practitioners: Jean Nicolas Corvisart (1755–1821) was a military surgeon and personal physician to Napoleon I. He performed "miracles" of diagnosis; with him observation replaced examination. Other Holmesian mind readers included Corvisart's pupil Baron Guillaume Dupuytren (1777–1835), Armand Trousseau (1801–67), and the pioneer dermatologist of sarcastic wit, Ferdinand von Hebra (1816–80). Even Sir Arbuthnot Lane published a number of papers on the marks of occupation on the human frame. But it was Joe Bell who incarnated this medical fine art for the young Doyle. Bell later recollected that young Arthur

> was amused once when a patient walked in and sat down. "Good morning, Pat," I said for it was impossible not to see that he was an Irishman. "Good morning, your honour," replied the patient. "Did you like your walk over the links to-day as you came in from the south side of the town?" I asked. "Yes," said Pat. "Did your honour see me?"
>
> Well, Conan Doyle could not see how I knew that, absurdly simple as it was.
>
> On a showery day, such as that had been, the reddish clay at bare parts of the links adheres to the boot and a tiny part is bound to remain. There is no such clay anywhere else round the town for miles. That and one or two similar instances excited Doyle's keenest interest and set him experimenting in the same directions, which, of course, was just what I wanted with all my other students.[27]

In these days of rapid, automated transit, the Holmesian diagnostician would probably need to take his clay samples from automobile tires.

Another example of Bell's art:

> "This man is a left-handed cobbler."
> "You'll obsairve, gentlemen, the worn places on the corduroy breeks

where a cobbler rests his lapstone? The right-hand side, you'll note, is far-r more worn than the left. He uses his left for hammering the leather."

Again:

"This man is a French-polisher."
"Come, now. Can't you smel-l-l him?"[28]

Again:

A woman with a small child was shown in. Joe Bell said good morning to her and she said good morning in reply.
"What sort of crossing di' ye have fra' Burntisland?"
"It was guid."
"And had ye a guid walk up Inverleith Row?"
"Yes."
"And what did ye do with th' other wain?"
"I left him with my sister in Leith."
"And would ye still be working at the linoleum factory?"
"Yes, I am."
"You see, gentlemen, when she said good morning to me I noted her Fife accent, and, as you know, the nearest town in Fife is Burntisland. You notice the red clay on the edges of the sole of her shoes, and the only such clay within twenty miles of Edinburgh is the Botanical Gardens. Inverleith Row borders the gardens and is her nearest way here from Leith. You observed that the coat she carried over her arm is too big for the child who is with her, and therefore she set out from home with two children. Finally she has dermatitis on the fingers of the right hand which is peculiar to workers in the linoleum factory at Burntisland."

And, probably the most famous:

"Well, my man, you've served in the Army?"
"Aye, sir."
"Not long discharged?"
"No sir."
"A Highland Regiment?"
"Aye, sir."
"A non-commissioned officer?"
"Aye, sir."
"Stationed at Barbadoes?"
"Aye, sir."
"You see, gentlemen, the man was a respectful man, but he did not remove his hat. They do not in the army, but he would have learned civilian ways had he been long discharged. He has an air of authority and he is obviously Scottish. As to Barbadoes, his complaint is elephantiasis,

which is West Indian and not British, and the Scottish regiments are at present in that particular island."[29]

This was mind reading or white magic; in the next generation, it would be replaced by the interpretation of dreams. It recalls the age-old unity of Aesculapian medicine, which originally was a mantic art.

"Try to learn the features of a disease or injury as precisely as you know the features, the gait, the tricks of manner of your most intimate friend. Him, even in a crowd, you can recognize at once. It may be a crowd of men dressed alike, and each having his full complement of eyes, nose, hair, and limbs. In every essential they resemble one another; only in trifles do they differ and yet, by knowing these trifles well, you make your recognition or your diagnosis with ease."[30] Trifles, signs and symptoms, clues—all were grist for Bell's diagnostic mill.

The emphasis on meticulous observation is traditional in medicine and has been repeated in many forms: "More is missed by not looking than by not knowing" (Thomas McCrac); "For one mistake made for not knowing, ten mistakes are made for not looking" (J. A. Lindsay);

> More harm is done because you do not look
> Than from not knowing what is in the book.[31]

This observational imperative requires, however, a long apprenticeship. "In the last analysis," said Charcot, "we see only what we are ready to see, what we have been taught to see. We eliminate and ignore everything that is not a part of our prejudices."[32] In this case, prejudice is not necessarily bad; the number of facts to be observed in a single still-life approaches infinity. Through the categories of experience and prejudice, meaning and intelligibility are imposed on the chaos of phenomena.

Bell's bravura performances were only elementary lessons for beginners. Time and experience were necessary to transform these novice physicians into practitioners of mature judgement. The possibility of error was always near at hand to humble the most brilliant diagnostician.

"You are a bandsman?"

"Aye," replied the sick man.

Dr. Bell cockily turned to his students, "You see, gentlemen, I am right. This man has a paralysis of his cheek muscles, the result of too much blowing at band instruments."

And turning again to the patient, "What instrument do you play, my man?"

"The big drum," came the reply.[33]

The impression that Joseph Bell made on Doyle was unique in the annals of medical education. Bedside teaching skills usually live on only in the clinical practice of students. Rarely has such a teaching style been so transformed—and immortalized. When Doyle wrote to Bell—"It is most certainly to you that I owe Sherlock Holmes, and although in the stories I have the advantage of being able to place him in all sorts of dramatic positions, I do not think that his analytical work is in the least an exaggeration of some effects which I have seen you produce in the out-patient ward"—Bell's response to Holmes as an alter ego included such descriptives as "cataract of drivel" and "heap of rubbish."[34] Doyle was not entirely unsympathetic to his old mentor's opinion, but Bell reportedly later grew reconciled to his fate and possibly was even secretly pleased.

THE AUTOCRATIC HOLMES

"Good morning, Holmes—what's your name?"
—Josiah Quincy

For high and dangerous action teaches us to believe as right beyond dispute things for which our doubting minds are slow to find words of proof.
—O. W. Holmes, Jr.

One of the most notable figures of the nineteenth century earned his professional reputation by the scientific application of deduction to the solution of a long series of mysterious deaths, although he rarely appeared in court to give evidence at criminal trials. His personal adventures, slightly disguised and appearing under a physician's by-line, almost singlehandedly made the reputation of one of the most popular periodicals of the day. He had annoying passions for chemistry and the violin, a strong interest in boxing, a fondness for lenses (the magnifying glass and the microscope), and an inclination to the meerschaum. His library contained innumerable works of reference, and he was himself more solitary than social but took great care to engineer his own public image.

The magazine whose reputation he established was *The Atlantic Monthly* and not *The Strand*, for this list of Sherlockian traits is actually a capsule biography of Oliver Wendell Holmes.[35] A pioneer of American medicine and letters, Holmes studied in Paris and returned with three principles: not to take authority when he could have facts, not to guess when he could know, and not to think a man must take physic because he is sick. His analytical approach to clinical problems produced the classic paper "The Contagiousness of Puerperal Fever" (1843), in which he anticipated Semmelweis by two decades in identifying the cause of childbed fever. Holmes was dean of the Harvard Medical School when Professor John Webster murdered Dr. George Parkman; in one of his rare courtroom appearances, his forensic evidence helped identify the victim's remains. A writer of occasional verse that has long survived its original stimulus, Holmes also had a conversational style that bordered on mind reading: "Holmes talks very nearly all the time but the secret of the charm of the monopoly is the fact that he is, all this time, *broidering on your woof*—apparently dwelling only on what you have suggested, and reading your mind very truly to yourself, only that he makes it seem a good deal clearer than you thought it!"[36] A very private individual, he fashioned his literary persona with careful deliberation: "I have come before the public like an actor who returns to fold his robes and make his bow to the audience."[37]

Holmes recognized that confidence is both appropriate to the professional and helpful to the patient: "Keep your doubts to yourself, and give the patient the benefit of your decision."[38] While a certain amount of bluff may be necessary—"Audacious self-esteem . . . is always imposing";[39] "The specialist is much like other people engaged in lucrative business. He is apt to magnify his calling, to make much of any symptom which will bring a patient within range of his battery of remedies"[40]—it can lead to both overdiagnosis and unnecessary treatment, if not outright charlatanism. The fifth physician to examine an infant with a simple cold may discover a pneumonia undetected by the previous four pediatricians. The anxious parents will be awed by this brilliant (mis)diagnostic coup, and the impression is reinforced that their baby's life has been saved only by the timely (albeit unnecessary) penicillin injection. Patients receiving dietotherapy for imaginary complaints will present a physician with their previous glucose tolerance test curves. When, after careful perusal, the practitioner informs them that all these laboratory results are normal, they respond, "Doctor Fiscalin D. Pendence warned us that other (namely, less competent) doctors would misinterpret it as normal."

As a professional medical educator, Holmes was committed to the scientific method and was a harsh critic of the many forms of imposture prevalent in the medicine of his day. As a man of letters, however, he understood that scientific facts did not begin to encompass the human domain with which medicine dealt. "All generous minds have a horror of what are commonly called 'facts.' They are the brute beasts of the intellectual domain. . . . Scientific knowledge. . . . has mingled with it a something which partakes of insolence. Absolute, peremptory facts are bullies, and those who keep company with them are apt to get a bullying habit of mind. There is no elasticity in a mathematical fact."[41]

Medicine needs a scientific base and method but can never become a pure science. Science can study the disease process but physicians treat patients not diseases. The humanist, Holmes, combined a belief in the necessity of a scientific approach with a certain skepticism with regard to the physician's ability to consistently distinguish science fact from personal opinion:

> Science is the topography of ignorance. From a few elevated points we triangulate vast spaces, inclosing infinite unknown details. We cast the lead, and draw up a little sand from abysses we may never reach with our dredges.
>
> The best part of our knowledge is that which teaches us where knowledge leaves off and ignorance begins. Nothing more clearly separates a vulgar from a superior mind, than the confusion in the first between the little that it truly knows, on the one hand, and what it half knows and what it thinks it knows on the other.[42]

Like Doyle and his detective hero, Dr. Holmes has a penchant for embedding subtle literary references in his occasional verse on mundane topics. Both doctors were in rebellion against the religion of their failed fathers (the Reverend Abiel Holmes had been dismissed by his congregation).[43] Faith in a materialistic determinism and rejection of a paternalistic providence are themes that pervade their writings (at least that part of Doyle's opera presently under consideration). They outlived the popularity of their doctrines and suffered a certain ingratitude on the part of their callous offspring (Sherlock Holmes/Justice Oliver Wendell Holmes, Jr.). Over time their essentially middle-class popularity with the common man became obscured; later generations would view these bourgeois writers as aristocrats and Brahmins.

William Osler recommended Holmes's Breakfast Table series as one of the ten works to be included in the physician's bedside library; that advice remains good today.

CHELM: THE PLACE OF ERROR IN MEDICAL EDUCATION

> A mythology reflects its region.
> —Wallace Stevens

The Medical Model

> The politics of emotion must appear
> To be an intellectual structure. The cause
> Creates a logic not to be distinguished
> From lunacy.
> —Wallace Stevens

> This is a case of my reasoning being, with one partial exception, perfectly correct. Everything I had deduced would no doubt have fitted the real owner of the clothes.
> —Maurice Baring, "From the Diary of Sherlock Holmes"

At the very time that medical student Doyle was falling under the influence of the brilliant Dr. Joseph Bell, there were stories current of less reputable practitioners utilizing a similar observation-and-deduction methodology. One example from the *Lancet* of 1892 has been reprinted in three medical journals as narrated by Dr. Lauder Brunton:

> An admirable example of the application to medicine of this method of tracking used to be told with great gusto by my late friend, Dr. Milner Fothergill, and I regret greatly that I cannot tell it with the same power and vividness that he did. In the town of Leeds there once lived a quack who had received no professional instruction whatever, but was known far and wide for his wonderful cures, and especially for his power of diagnosing the diseases of patients whom he had never seen, by simply examining their urine. A celebrated surgeon, Mr. X—, wishing to see his method of working, desired to be presented one day, and the quack readily acceded to his request, feeling much flattered that so great a man should patronize him. Shortly after Mr. X— had taken his seat, a woman came in with a bottle of urine, which she handed to the quack. He looked at her, then at the bottle, held it up between him and the light, shook it, and said:
> "Your husband's?"
> "Yes, sir."
> "He is a good deal older than you?"
> "Yes, sir."
> "He is a tailor?"
> "Yes, sir."
> "He lives at Scarcroft?"
> "Yes, sir."
> "His bowels are obstinate?"
> "Yes, sir."
> "Here," he said, handing her a box of pills, "tell him to take one of these pills every night for a week, and a big drink of cold water every morning, and he will soon be all right."
> No sooner had the woman gone out than Mr. X— turned to the quack, curious to know how he had made out all this.

"Well, you see," said the quack, "she was a young woman, and looked well and strong, and I guessed the water was not hers. As I saw she had a wedding ring on her finger, I knew she was married and I thought the chances were it was her husband's water. If he had been about the same age as she was it was hardly likely that he was going to be ill either, so I guessed he was older. I knew he was a tailor because the bottle was not stopped with a cork, but with a bit of paper rolled up and tied around with a thread in the way that no one but a tailor could have done it. Tailors get no exercise, and consequently are all very apt to be constipated. I was quite sure that he would be no exception to the rule, and so I gave him opening pills."

"But how did you know she came from Scarcroft?"

"Oh, Mr. X—, have you lived so long in Leeds and you don't know the color of Scarcroft clay? It was the first thing I saw on her boots the moment she came in."

Now, of late years we have got so many new methods of investigation that we are sometimes apt to forget the old habits of close observation by which this quack made out so much, and proved himself, although without any diploma, a worthy descendant of the water doctor whose picture by Gerard Dow occupies such a distinguished place in the gallery of the Louvre.[44]

These brilliant deductions impress medical students and lay people but, as in the case reported here, are totally independent of the practitioner's honesty or true medical ability.[45]

Holmesian deduction from meticulous observation has been criticized directly and indirectly from a number of perspectives. The best anticipatory criticism came from the mythical shtetl of Chelm, a town whose inhabitants were legendary for their stupidity. Their anti-intellectual transvaluation of all values is not as literarily refined as in the antirational tales of Nahman of Bratslav, but the moral of virtue and goodness residing in innocence and simplicity is just as clearly expressed. Dr. Magnesia of Chelm visits the doctor of a neighboring town for some postgraduate study. Since he persistently misdiagnoses cases, he goes to learn Dr. Smartest's method of diagnosis by observation: a man with a stomach ache has been eating too much canned food (many empty tin cans were observed outside the house), a small boy with a stomachache has eaten green apples (the apple cores were observed in the orchard), a woman with a backache has been rearranging furniture (new furniture was observed in the house). He then proceeds to misapply his lesson by interpreting a horse's harness under the bed of a man with a stomachache as proof that the patient has eaten a horse![46]

Another Chelmite employs age, dress, and time to successfully (?) solve a case of identity:

The Medical Model   35

A young man from Chelm was traveling to Pinsk to see his fiancee.
No sooner was he seated in the train than the stranger next to him said:
"So you are Mottle, the son of my good friend, Zalmen, and you're going to see Rifke." The stranger scrutinized him carefully and said: "Ah, Zalman has a fine-looking son. I'm glad for Zalman. And Rifke will have a good husband."
The Young man was mystified. "Yes, I am Zalmen's son and I'm going to Pinsk to see my fiancee, and I plan to propose to her. But how did you know all this? I have never seen you."
"Neither have I seen you, Mottle," said the stranger, "but what I told you is as plain as the nose on your face. You see that brief case you carry—the one you are holding on your lap."
"Yes, yes," said Mottle, impatiently.
"Well," said the stranger.
"Well," said Mottle.
"It's simple."
"Well, go on," said Mottle.
"Only a lawyer would carry a brief case. And I know you're from Chelm. And I think—I know Chelm a little—who in all Chelm has a son who is a lawyer? It doesn't take much thinking, for how many lawyers are there in all Chelm but one. And I know my friend, Zalmen, has a son who is a lawyer.
"And what would a young man be doing away from his work and traveling from his home on a weekday? The only such person would be a man in love. So I think. I know Pinsk much better than I do Chelm. Who would be a proper match? You could not be marrying Bebble. She is too old. Nor Sarah, her family would not be right for you; she is too low in class. So the only proper one left is Rifke. She is the right age and she is the doctor's daughter. It equals. It comes our perfectly."
"How remarkable!" said Mottle, Zalmen's son. "Unbelievable!"
The stranger shrugged his shoulders. "It's nothing. Nothing at all. It's simple, as plain as day—like the nose on your face. If one carries a brief case like you, to what other figure can one come?"[47]

In the *Boston Medical and Surgical Journal* for 26 May 1904, Dr. Courtney published an interesting parody of Sherlockian deduction, "Dr. Watson and Mr. Holmes; or the worm that turned." The Chelmite Watson takes Holmes on medical rounds and demonstrates the fallaciousness of the apparently obvious in clinical diagnosis. Watson first asks the externe to show in the musician:

"I'm sorry, sir," said the externe, "but I haven't had time to take any histories, and I don't know who you mean."
Watson walked to the door, threw it open, and beckoned to a man sitting on the front seat. The patient entered and sat before Watson's table.
"Musician, did you say?" asked Holmes apathetically.

"Yes, musician, and I should add, a player on a wind instrument."

Holmes examined the man's buccinators in their normal condition, and then got him to puff out his cheeks. He appeared satisfied with his examination, and when Watson asked him if he had made up his mind as to how he, Watson, had arrived at his conclusion as to the man's occupation, he answered in a tired way, "Why, certainly, you have only to look at the muscles of his lips and cheeks; they tell the story."

"Wrong," said Watson; "it's much simpler than that. Just observe the little goatee he wears. I venture to say he believes the loss of that would prevent his playing for a week. Am I right?" he asked, turning to the man.

"Oh, yes, sir. I wouldn't cut that off for the world; it's strengthening to the lip, and I shouldn't be able to play till it grew again."

Watson soon got at the facts of the case, examined and disposed of it.

During this time Holmes looked absently out of the window.

The next patient was ushered in, and without speaking, presented a note to Watson. The latter, without looking at the note, exclaimed, "Ah, a teamster, I see."

"That observation was superfluous," broke in Holmes superciliously. "I knew he was a teamster the moment I saw him. He has the complexion of a man much exposed to the weather and wears the sort of clothes common to people of that class."

"That may all be true, but it would apply equally well to a cabman; and it is dangerous to draw conclusions on such general grounds. Perhaps you did not notice that this man took the note he brought me out of his hat—a typical teamster trick."

Holmes made no reply, but bit his lips furiously while Watson read the note. Watson turned the case over to his assistant and called for the next patient. It proved to be a man with a marked tremor of the right hand. Without a word, Watson took hold of the trembling hand and observed it closely for a few moments. Then he said quietly, "Here, my dear Holmes, is an interesting tremor in a left-handed plasterer, who has done no work for some time. Am I right, my man?"

"Quite right, sir," was the answer. "I'm left-handed and I'm a plasterer by trade, but this cursed shaking has laid me up for nearly six months now." At this point Holmes was about to say something, but hesitated and looked the man over carefully in silence. Watson sat quietly back in his chair and observed his friend's scrutiny of the patient with an amused twinkle in his eye.

Holmes' face was a study. It had grown several shades yellower than usual, and again made Watson think of pernicious anemia. The powerful magnifying lens was now brought into play and the man's nails, ears and eyebrows thoroughly examined by its aid. Obviously Holmes was stumped. By this time he was breathing hard and mopping his brow.

After a time Watson broke in with: "Well, my dear Holmes, what do you say?"

"Nothing, except that it's beastly stuffy in this room," growled Sherlock, the peerless.

"Well, let's have a window open, and then, perhaps, I can show you a thing or two of interest about this man that you may have overlooked with your glass. You will first observe that the tremor involves the right hand. On looking at this hand closely, you will see a half-softened callus over each joint of the thumb, and similar ones over the root joint and the one next to it of the forefinger. You see none over any other joints. This shows that these particular joints mentioned must habitually come in contact with some hard surface. Now, from my study of artisans' hands, I know that this condition is peculiar to the plasterer, and that it is brought about by the contact of the mortar board. In this case it is the right hand that shows the condition, so the man must do the actual plastering with the left. I hardly need mention that the somewhat softened condition of the calluses indicates this man's abstinence from work for some time."

While Watson was engaged in demonstrating the reasons for his conclusions, Holmes paced rapidly up and down the room, apparently paying not the slightest attention. Finally he whipped out his watch, looked at it, and said, "By Jove, Watson, I must go. I've got an important engagement that I had almost forgotten."

"Oh, don't be in such an infernal rush," replied the doctor. "I've got to get away early myself. I'll tell you what I'll do. I'll just turn this man over to my assistant, see the next case or two hurriedly, and then go along with you."

At Watson's order the next case was led in. "This man," said the externe, "is a rubbercutter, and his complaint is of headache and dizziness."

"Now, Holmes," said the doctor, "won't you just look at this fellow's gums with your glass and see if you don't see a dark line at the junction of the gums and teeth. You do—thank you. It's a clear case of lead poisoning, just as I thought. Now, my man, let me look at your tongue."

A sudden exclamation from Holmes caused Watson to look at him. As he did so he noticed that his friend's face had suddenly taken on an expression very like what one might expect to see in a mummy that had been spoiled in the making. "Did you speak?" he asked, somewhat maliciously.

"No," growled Holmes between his clenched teeth, "but the diagnosis in this case is too absurdly clear. This man has either been doing some painting at home, or else he uses a hair wash containing lead. Isn't that so, my good fellow?" asked Sherlock, addressing the patient.

"Aw, I never washes me hair," was the reply; "and I have enough to do in the shop without bothering with no painting at home. It ain't in my line."

Holmes collapsed in his chair.

"Perhaps if he will tell us just what his functions as a rubber-cutter are, it will help you to arrive at a correct solution of the problem," put in the doctor, dryly. "Exactly what is your work, my man?"

"I just puts the patterns down on the sheet rubber and cuts around them with a knife," was the answer.

"Does that help you, Holmes?" asked Watson.

The great detective sat dejectedly and made no reply.

"Well, we won't waste any more time on it," rattled on Watson, "but the situation is just this. From your extensive reading and observations, you must know that in the preparation of rubber there is used a considerable amount of litharge, or the red oxide of lead. Now you don't have to examine this fellow's hands very closely to conclude that soap is not a large factor in his items of expenditure. My glance at his tongue showed me that he is an habitual tobacco chewer. On the basis of these two observations, I concluded that the transference of really considerable amounts of the lead from fingers to mouth was a daily occurrence.[48]

With experience to bolster his limited powers of observation and deduction, Watson does to Holmes what Holmes typically does to the Metropolitan Police; the lessons are not different, the shoe is merely on the other foot. Apart from the fact that in Doyle's stories Watson never exhibited any hint of the most basic skills of observation and deduction, what this role reversal really demonstrates is the preeminence of clinical experience over the required (but minimal) superficium of abstract deductive logic that is frequently confused with science.

Individuals are unique and react differently to the same disease process. Commenting on the appropriateness to medicine of Butler's axiom "Probability is the guide of life," William Osler offered the following example of a detailed (but erroneous) sequence of observations and conclusion:

Surrounded by people who demand certainty, and not philosopher enough to agree with Locke that "Probability supplies the defect of our knowledge and guides us when that fails and is always conversant about things of which we have no certainty," the practitioner too often gets into a habit of mind which resents the thought that opinion, not full knowledge, must be his stay and prop. There is no discredit, though there is at times much discomfort, in this everlasting *perhaps* with which we have to preface so much connected with the practice of our art. It is, as I said, inherent in the subject. Take in illustration an experience of last week. I saw a patient with Dr. Bolgiano who presented marked pulsation to the left of the sternum in the second, third and fourth interspaces, visible even before the night-dress was removed, a palpable impulse over the area of pulsation, flatness on percussion, accentuated heart sounds and a soft systolic bruit. When to this were added paralysis of the left recurrent laryngeal nerve, smallness of the radial pulse on the left side, and tracheal tugging, there is not one of you who would not make, under such circumstances, the diagnosis of aneurism of the aorta. Few of us, indeed, would put in the *perhaps,* or think of it as a probability with such a combination of physical signs, and yet the associate conditions which had been present—a small primary tumour of the left lobe of the thyroid, with secondary nodules in the lymph glands of the neck and involvement of the mediastinum and tumour causing the remarkable intrathoracic combination was not aneurismal but malignant. Listen to the appropriate comment of the Father of Medicine, who twenty-five centuries ago had not only grasped the fundamental conception of our art as one based on observation, but had laboured also through a long life to give to the profession which he loved the saving health of science—listen, I say to words of his famous aphorism: "Experience is fallacious and judgment difficult!" [italics deleted]49

The exaggeration of Holmes's deductive powers frequently borders on absurdity. Doyle corrects this impression by documenting many false trails followed, missed clues, premature hypotheses, and erroneous conclusions. Although an occasional client is buried, a fair number of mismanaged cases are solved in spite of these logical errors, which are more often due to "the overrefinement of his logic—his preference for a subtle and bizarre explanation when a plainer and more commonplace one lay ready at hand" *(The Sign of Four)*. It is a medical maxim that common diseases cause uncommon symptoms more often than uncommon diseases cause common symptoms.

The status of "The Yellow Face" as the great detective's most clear-cut failure needs to be reassessed. Holmes's preliminary hypothesis of blackmail is quite valid, despite Watson's reservations:

"What do you think of my theory?"
"It is all surmise."
"But at least it covers all the facts. When new facts come to our knowledge which cannot be covered by it, it will be time enough to reconsider it."

But it is entirely the product of history taking; there is no physical examination; when firsthand data are later sought, they are obtained directly by the client and yield an immediate denouement to the case (see Figure 1). Many details are left unresolved and have led to much speculation with regard to other possible solutions—"one can always conceive alternative explanations" ("The Problem of Thor Bridge"). However, this relatively superficial reading of "The Yellow Face" does not do it justice, and a more detailed investigation of its structure may prove rewarding. A careful review of the opening framing sequence at 221 B Baker Street allows a somewhat different interpretation of this tangled tale. Aristotle noted that in dramatic prologues and in epic poetry, a foretaste of the theme should be given in advance instead of keeping the audience in complete suspense. Just as Holmes's apparent failure to solve the case hinges on his lack of any firsthand physical evidence, so his initial analysis of his client's character is completed before he ever sets eyes on Mr. Grant Munro. From an inspection of

		PRESENT
PAST Effie Hebron		Effie Munro
John Hebron	Lucy Hebron	strange behavior
death certificate		(money request)

Figure 1. "The Yellow Face"

Holmes correctly traces the cause of Mrs. Munro's strange behavior to something from out of her past. The unusual request for a large sum of money suggests the possibility of blackmail, so Holmes quite legitimately hypothesizes that the late Mr. Hebron's death certificate may be false: a live ex-husband would threaten Effie's current marital status. The detective blunders by not applying the lesson of "Silver Blaze": the failure of the dog to bark is quite analogous to the absence of little Lucy's death certificate. It is not her first husband's survival that Effie wants concealed from her second husband but rather his race, a fact quite clearly revealed by Lucy's skin pigmentation. The crime in this most peculiar narrative would appear to be one of self-blackmail.

Mr. Munro's pipe alone, it may be concluded that its owner is a creature of habit who prefers to keep old used things rather than replace them with new ones. The pipe has two silver rings and is charred down one side from its previous mode of being lit, which also identifies its owner as, in some way, sinister. These deductions from the pipe have all but summarized the entire plot of the tale that follows; all that remains is to clarify the client's identity, which Holmes proceeds to do by the not very subtle trick of reading his name from an exposed hat lining.

Holmes's description of the pipe and its owner matches the story line in the same way that a (?pipe) dream distorts the reality on which it is based. All the elements are there; it merely remains to see them in the right perspective. Although Holmes is not instrumental in solving the case (as more often than not a patient's recovery is independent of any medical intervention), he maintains a professionally supportive role throughout. With the goal of bringing "peace to many troubled souls," he reassures—"and above all things do not fret until you know that you really have a cause for it"—and counsels pursuing a definitive diagnosis—"Any truth is better than indefinite doubt." Doyle's handling of deductive errors and the limitations of science may be a more accurate reflection of his medical models than his finest examples of detective skills.

Holmes stresses observation as the basis of his new science of detection; Gargantua placed the faculty of observation at the foundation of his new scheme of pedagogy for the young Pantagruel. The roots of puzzle literature might be traced to the kennings of the ancient skalds, but there are stronger influences from the *Halsrätsel*, or "capital riddle," in which the detective—a Gawain or an Oedipus—must solve the riddle or forfeit his head. Sherlock Holmes is not an ivory-tower academic researcher; he risks action in a world of intense physical danger. Often such decisive action redeems otherwise inexcusable logical failures. The next chapter will investigate some of the nonmedical antecedents of Sherlock Holmes.

4
Literary Archetypes

> How simply the fictive hero becomes the real.
> —Wallace Stevens

> A learned plagiary of all the others;
> You track him everywhere in their snow.
> —Dryden, "Essay of Dramatic Poesy"

> It's all been done before, and will be again.
> —*The Valley of Fear*

DUPIN'S DECEPTION

> The moral activity which *disentangles* . . .
> —Poe

> There is nothing more unaesthetic than a policeman.
> —*The Sign of the Four*

> Someone may observe that no doubt the conclusion preceded the "proofs."
> —Jorge Luis Borges

Edgar Allan Poe was a minor American poet and critic who also wrote fantastic tales. A fine ear for the sound of language combined with occasional flashes of insight to produce several amazing and enduring works, but his eccentricity and egotism hindered his achieving classic stature. When Lowell said that Poe was three-fifths genius and two-fifths sheer fudge, he was charitably underestimating the fudge component.

It is on the basis of four of his short stories that Poe is frequently considered to be the inventor of the literary detective story; these tales of ratiocination include "The Gold Bug" (1843), "The Murders in the Rue Morgue" (1841), "The Mystery of Marie Roget" (1842), and "The Purloined Letter" (1845).[50] Three of these narratives chronicle the adventures of the Parisian chevalier C. Auguste Dupin, while the fourth (GB) is essentially an exercise in cryptography by one William Legrand of French Huguenot extraction. Dupin performs four spectacular feats: (1) he solves a brutal, motiveless locked-room murder (RM) by a meticulous attention to detail, especially the resolution of conflicting ear-witness testimony; (2) he resolves conflicting newspaper theories of a murder (MR); (3) he repeats the substitution of the purloined letter (PL); (4) he reads the mind of his narrator/companion (RM). In GB, Legrand solves the cipher that leads to the discovery of Captain Kidd's treasure.

Many of the standard traits of the detective-hero are clearly foreshadowed in these stories and certainly influenced Conan Doyle's characterization of Sherlock Holmes. The most obvious similarities include:

Eccentric character:	"stricken with lunacy" (GB)
	"madmen of a harmless nature" (RM)
	"the rather fantastic gloom of our common temper" (RM)
Cold and callous:	"frigid and abstract" (RM)
	"he seemed not so much sulky as abstracted" (GB)
Superhuman intellectual powers:	"exhibiting in his solutions of each a degree of *acumen* which appears to the ordinary apprehension praeternatural" (RM)
	"the affair was regarded as little less than miraculous" (MR)
Enthusiasm over latest scientific discoveries:	GB
A specific address:	au troisieme, No. 33 Rue Dunot, Faubourg St. Germaine (PL)
Meticulous observer:	"He makes in silence a host of observations and inferences";
	"The necessary knowledge is that of *what* to observe." (RM)

Split (schizophrenic) personality:	"subject to perverse moods of alternate enthusiasm and melancholy" (GB)
Tobacco addict:	"I was enjoying the twofold luxury of meditation and a meerschaum"; "'True,' said Dupin, after a long and thoughtful whiff from his meerschaum"; "'Why, yes,' said Dupin, drawlingly between the whiffs of his meerschaum"; "intently and exclusively occupied with the curling eddies of smoke that oppressed the atmosphere of the chamber." (PL)
Bachelor	
Platonic male roommate:	"we should live together during my stay in the city." (RM)
Bewildered (mentally inferior) admirer	
Physician narrator:	"Allow me this once to prescribe for you"; "Follow my advice implicitly, as that of your physician." (GB)
Mind-reading trick:	RM
Multilingual:	quotes Latin, German, French
Theater buff:	RM
Interest in codes:	Poe's reputation as a cryptanalyst had little foundation and was greatly exaggerated (by himself). His "air of method" masked an inductive and intuitive approach that was imaginative but unscientific. Poe's assumption that all codes could be broken— "It may well be doubted whether human ingenuity can construct an enigma of the kind which human ingenuity may not, by proper application, resolve" (GB)—has suffered the fate of many poetic insights into the realm of scientific truth and is now known to be incorrect.[51]
Bibliophile:	"Books, indeed, were his sole luxuries" (RM) "He had with him many books" (GB)

Literary Archetypes 45

Materialist:	refuses to accept nonnatural explanations (GB, RM)
Broad range of interests:	"a comprehension of *all* the sources whence legitimate advantage may be derived" (RM)
Dark milieu:	"enamored of the night for her own sake"; "The sable divinity would not herself dwell with us always; but we could counterfeit her presence." (RM)
Interest in puzzles:	"He is fond of enigmas, of conundrums, hieroglyphics"; "An inquiry will afford us amusement" (RM)
Flair for (melo)dramatic:	"a little bit of sober mystification" (GB)
Exaggerated boasting:	"I have solved others of an abstruseness ten thousand times greater"; "the extravagant demeanor of Legrand" (GB)
Archenemy:	Minister D- has a reputation as a mathematician and can be confused with his brother(s). "'But is this really the poet?' I asked. 'There are two brothers, I know; and both have attained reputation in letters. The minister I believe has written learnedly on the Differential Calculus. He is a mathematician, and no poet.'" (PL; the points of similarity with Professor Moriarity are striking.)
Bumbling and incompetent police bureaucracy	
A method:	Dorothy Sayers remarked that "Murders in the Rue Morgue" constituted a complete manual of literary detective theory and practice. From "imperfect observation to intuition that is the idiosyncrasy of the individual man of genius" (MR), the analytic approach is itself "little susceptible of analysis" (RM). Several of Poe's practical rules for detection include a principle of noncontradiction: "All apparent impos-

	sibilities *must* be proved to be not such in reality" (RM).
Imaginative psychology:	the detective must be able to "throw himself into the spirit of his opponent" by an "identification of the reasoner's intellect with that of his opponent." (RM)
Circumstantial evidence:	Collateral threads, seemingly irrelevant, incidental, or accidental details, are potentially significant: "*Accident* is admitted as a portion of the substructure. We make chance a matter of absolute calculation" (MR). Poe's attempt at an intuitive mathematical justification of such evidence via probability theory is, at the least, clumsy and unconvincing.
Sociology:	Popular opinion or rumor always has a foundation in fact. (GB, MR) The *outré*: paradoxically, it is the unusual or bizarre features of a crime (the "deviations from the plane of ordinary" [RM], "prominences above the plane of the ordinary" [MR]) that make it easier to solve when the "proper question" is asked: "What has occurred that has never occurred before?" (MR)

With this handful of limited insights, Poe attempted to apply his "method" to a sensational unsolved New York murder. Sayers ranked Poe among that "small band of mystery writers who have put their skill in deduction to the acid test of a problem which they had not in the first place invented."[52] Mary Rogers was killed in 1841; Poe's solution to this real mystery began serialization in 1842 with the lame hypothesis of first-degree murder by a naval officer. Before the final installment, in 1843 evidence came forward to support a verdict of death from criminal abortion. By a series of subtle last-minute additions and deletions to his manuscript (with several further revisions prior to its inclusion in his 1845 *Tales*), Poe perpetrated his "greatest hoax": the final revision of the text gives the impression that Poe correctly touched on the correct solution, while in reality his speculations were totally wrong. Having uncovered this fraud, the literary detective John Walsh concluded, "I have tried hard to find some mitigating reason for Poe's putting forth such an obviously false claim. He was not at heart a conscious and deliberate liar, but was of the type that finds it easy to make large and sweeping pronouncements from the slimmest justification and merest coincidences."[53] Whatever the excuses offered, Poe's attempt at real detective work was a dismal failure in contrast to Conan Doyle's more successful forays into the realm of criminal justice. This dishonest pose must unfortunately, but revealingly, head the list of significant differences between Poe's detectives and Sherlock Holmes:

Author a failure in real-life detection	
No other cases:	"the cases were not few in which attempt was made to engage his services at the Prefecture." (MR)
Prefers inactivity:	"his indolent humor", "old habits of moody reverie" (MR); "the energy of his character succumbed . . . and he ceased to bestir himself in the world, or to care for the retrieval of his fortunes." (RM)
Candid about past:	"I was deeply interested in the little family history which he detailed to me with all that candor which a Frenchman indulges whenever mere self is the theme." (RM) Of an illustrious family, reduced to poverty (GB, RM)
Poet:	"I have been guilty of certain doggerel myself." (PL)
Newspapers:	Although Dupin uses newspapers for advertisement (RM) and analysis (MR), he tends to avoid them: "it had been nearly a month since either of us had . . . more than glanced at the leading political activities in one of the daily papers" (MR). Neither Poe nor Doyle ever achieved that critical spirit with regard to the popular press that William Osler deemed necessary for the physician: "Believe nothing that you see in the newspapers. . . . If you

Narrator as equal:	see anything in them that you know is true begin to doubt it at once." Dupin's narrator provides much more of the theoretical background than Dr. Watson; at times the stories almost degenerate into anonymous lectures. Also, the narrator is actively involved in other of Dupin's work: "Engaged in researches which had absorbed our whole attention." (MR)
Social isolate:	"infected with misanthropy" (GB) "Our seclusion was perfect. We admitted no visitors.... We existed within ourselves alone" (RM)
Short-sighted:	green glassed spectacles (MR)
Motivation:	Despite the claim that "My ultimate object is only the truth" (RM), the true motivations appear to be repaying a favor (RM), greed (MR, GB), and revenge (PL).

Sherlock Holmes would have preferred his cases to be recorded as scientific treatises and disparaged Watson's romanticized narratives. If Watson had been able to comply with Holmes's wishes, he would have produced nonadventures as tediously dull and pretentious as the literary reconstruction of Mary Rogers's murder. Poe's criticism, his tales, even his poetry tended to be lectures or examples of the abstract principles expressed in such lectures. Discussing "The Raven" in his "Philosophy of Composition" (1846), Poe experimented with criticobabble: "It is my design to render it manifest that no one point in its composition is referable either to accident or intuition—that the work proceeded step by step, to its completion, with the precision and rigid consequence of a mathematical problem."[54] His oeuvre preached a repetitious sermon with one solitary moral: Edgar Allan Poe was a genius of the first order.

It would be a pardonable oversimplification to conclude that Poe lacked the humility necessary to create a character with an independent life. The author was too insecure to allow such competition with his work. Poe had a logical reason (of course) for the brevity of Dupin's career: "When . . . I endeavored, about a year ago, to depict some very remarkable features in the mental character of my friend, the Chevalier C. Auguste Dupin, it did not occur to me that I should ever resume the subject. This depicting of character constituted my design; and this design was thoroughly fulfilled in the wild train of circumstances brought to instance Dupin's idiosyncrasy. I should have proven no more." (MR) There is a deceptive modesty in this ratiocination over and above the deception that makes up the very essence of the literary fraud of Marie Roget: it is not so much that Dupin could have no other adventures to increase readers' appreciation of his genius as that the principles already exhibited should suffice to prove Edgar Allan Poe's preeminence.

Although his own eccentric aesthetic prevented him from fully realizing its import and his hero Dupin was a creature of dubious motives, there is one last aspect of the detective hero that Doyle was to find echoed in Poe's work and that would become one of the most distinguishing characteristics of Sherlock Holmes. Despite much pretence toward a scientific philosophy, Poe saw in the mechanized scientific method for grinding out truths a significant threat to individual creativity. When he quoted Landor in a footnote to Marie Roget, he almost—but not quite—perceived the necessary connection between such creative genius (the *true*, both abstract and concrete) and justice (the *good*): "when law becomes a science and a system, it ceases to be justice." Doyle and Holmes were to make an immortal and impassioned career of fighting all such systems—following a lead in a footnote to a piece of literary fudge.

THE MISERABLE BUNGLER LECOQ

> Above all, regard with supreme suspicion that which seems probable and begin always by believing what seems incredible.
> —Emile Gaboriau

> When once you have taken the impossible into your calculations its possibilities become practically limitless.
> —Saki

Emile Gaboriau was born between 1833 and 1835. After serving as a cavalry officer, he became a writer-humorist and achieved fame as the creator of two fictional detectives, the amateur Père Tabaret and the professional Monsieur Lecoq. His characters possessed many of the standard trappings of the great detective: the shrewd observation; brilliant logical deductions; the mastery of disguise; reading footprints (complete with plaster casts); the identification of tobacco ashes; the bumbling, bewildered admirer; and the professional jealousy and antagonism of the official detective corps. Despite these innovations, Gaboriau's tales are presented as novels rather than short stories, with plots hanging on remote family scandals that are laboriously revealed in long and tedious flashbacks—a device that Doyle unhappily imitated in *A Study in Scarlet* and *The Valley of Fear*.[55]

According to his Boswell, Father Absinthe, Tabaret is an amateur detective, a bibliomaniac in the literature of crime and police lore; he "devoured them as Don Quixote did the books of chivalry." For Tabaret detection is a mixture of scientific investigation—"the solution of a problem"—with the thrill of the hunt—"Give me the hunting of a man! . . . The game in my sport is worth the hunter"—as they present to an aesthetic sensibility—"the art is being lost because fine crimes are rare." Gaboriau's professional detective was part of the establishment, a member of Vidocq's Sûreté, and in many ways he was closer to Vidocq than to Holmes.

Lecoq's popularity required that his adventures continue beyond the career of his creator. Fortune de Boisgobey (1824–91) recounted the exploits of Lecoq's old age after Gaboriau's early death.

FRANÇOIS EUGÈNE VIDOCQ

That man is all best who himself works out every problem
—Hesiod

The hero is a feeling, a man seen
As if the eye was an emotion,
As if in seeing we saw our feeling
In the object seen and saved that mystic
Against the sight, the penetrating,
Pure eye.
—Wallace Stevens

Vidocq was a criminal turned policeman whose goal was to found a new profession, that of the scientific detective. He headed the Brigade de la Sûreté from its inception in 1812, and when he retired from the official police, he opened the world's first private detective agency, the Information Bureau, on 3 January 1834.

Vidocq mixed fact and fantasy in his *Memoires* (1828) and several later collections of exaggerated exploits; his friends Dumas and Eugene Sue used him as a character in a number of their writings. He pioneered in the use of handwriting analysis, fingerprints, footprints, ballistics, blood tests, and autopsy results. Apart from forensic science, he employed psychological insight to anticipate a criminal's moves, and to reflect his own encyclopedic memory, compiled criminal files combining physical descriptions with modus operandi and personal idiosyncrasies.

Although his innovative contributions to criminology were extensive, with his flair for the theater and a genius for disguise, he seemed always intent on creating a great romantic persona. Theatricality was mixed with secrecy to the extent that it was almost impossible to determine the truth about his exploits. This was not simply flamboyant posturing but effective crime-fighting by cowing the underworld into believing him and his plainclothes detectives to be infallible; he spread contradictory rumors about himself to keep his enemies off guard. As a private investigator, he would sometimes impress prospective clients by an exhibition of mind reading:

> On how many occasions have I not overwhelmed with amazement the persons who came to complain of any robbery! Scarcely had they related two or three circumstances, when I was immediately in possession of the whole facts; I concluded their story; or, without waiting for more explanations, I said, *"the thief is so and so."* They were thunderstruck.[56]

Having thrived in one of the most turbulent periods of French history, he lived an active life to a peaceful and wealthy end.

D'ARTAGNAN DETECTIVE

> They are characters beyond
> Reality, composed thereof. They are
> The fictive man created out of men.
> They are men but artificial men. They are
> Nothing in which it is not possible
> To believe . . .
> —Wallace Stevens

> Except in the life of a hero, the whole world's meaningless. The hero sees values beyond what's possible. That's the *nature* of a hero . . .
> —John Gardner, *Grendel*

D'Artagnan, the eighteen-year-old Gascon boaster, courageous swordsman, compulsive duelist, and righter of wrongs, was introduced in Alexandre Dumas's *Three Musketeers* (1844), returned in *Twenty Years After* (1845), and made his final appearance in *The Vicomte de Bragelonne ou dix ans plus tard* (1848–50). This enthusiastic adventurer and loyal comrade matures through a turbulent period of Franco-European history only to die just as he is finally rewarded with the Marshal's baton—*le bâton brodé de fleurs de lis d'or*—with his last words incomprehensible to his troops—"*Athos, Porthos, au revoir.—Aramis, à jamais adieu!*" The second volume of *The Vicomte de Bragelonne* provides not only D'Artagnan's exitus (chapter 113) but also the somewhat unexpected portrait of D'Artagnan the detective (chapters 20, 21).

Louis XIV sends D'Artagnan to the Rond-point du Bois-Rochin to investigate a wounded man and a dead horse. After a half hour of meticulous observation, D'Artagnan returns to Fontainebleu and delivers his report "as far as probability goes."

"Sire, your majesty told me that there was a horse lying dead in the cross-road of the Bois-Rochin, and I began, therefore, by studying the roads. I say the roads, because the center of the cross-road is reached by four separate roads. The one that I myself took was the only one that presented any fresh traces. Two horses had followed it side by side; their eight feet were marked very distinctly in the clay. One of the riders was more impatient than the other, for the footprints of the one were invariably in advance of the other about half a horse's length."

"Are you quite sure they were traveling together?" said the king.

"Yes, sire. The horses were two rather large animals of equal pace,—horses well used to maneuvers of all kinds, for they wheeled round the barrier of the Rond-point together."

"Well—and after?"

"The two cavaliers paused there for a minute, no doubt to arrange the conditions of the engagement; the horses grew restless and impatient. One of the riders spoke, while the other listened and seemed to have contented himself by simply answering. His horse pawed the ground, which proves that his attention was so taken up by listening that he let the bridle fall from his hand."

"A hostile meeting did take place then?"

"Undoubtedly."

"Continue; you are a very accurate observer."

"One of the two cavaliers remained where he was standing, the one, in fact, who had been listening; the other crossed the open space, and at first placed himself directly opposite to his adversary. The one who had remained stationary traversed the Rond-point at a gallop, about two-thirds of its length, thinking that by this means he would gain upon his opponent; but the latter had followed the circumference of the wood."

"You are ignorant of their names, I suppose."

"Completely so, sire. Only he who followed the circumference of the wood was mounted on a black horse."

"How do you know that?"

"I found a few hairs of his tail among the brambles which bordered the sides of the ditch."

"Go on."

"As for the other horse, there can be no trouble in describing him, since he was left dead on the field of battle."

"What was the cause of his death?"

"A ball which had passed through his brain."

"Was the ball that of a pistol or a gun?"

"It was a pistol-bullet, sire. Besides, the manner in which the horse was wounded explained to me the tactics of the man who had killed it. He had followed the circumference of the wood in order to take his adversary in flank. Moreover, I followed his foot-tracks on the grass."

"The tracks of the black horse, do you mean?"

"Yes, sire."

"Go on, Monsieur d'Artagnan."

"As your majesty now perceives the position of the two adversaries, I will, for a moment, leave the cavalier who had remained stationary for the one who started off at a gallop."

"Do so."

"The horse of the cavalier who rode at full speed was killed on the spot."

"How do you know that?"

"The cavalier had not time even to throw himself off his horse, and so fell with it. I observed the impression of his leg, which, with a great effort, he was enabled to extricate from under the horse. The spur, pressed down by the weight of the animal, had plowed up the ground."

"Very good; and what did he do as soon as he rose up again?"

"He walked straight up to his adversary."

"Who still remained upon the verge of the forest?"

"Yes, sire. Then, having reached a favorable distance, he stopped firmly, for the impression of both his heels are left in the ground quite close to each other, fired, and missed his adversary."

"How do you know he did not hit him?"

"I found a hat with a ball through it."

"Ah, a proof, then!" exclaimed the king.

"Insufficient, sire," replied D'Artagnan, coldly; "it is a hat without any letters indicating its ownership, without arms; a red feather, as all hats have; the lace, even, had nothing particular in it."

"Did the man with the hat through which the bullet had passed fire a second time?"

"Oh, sire, he had already fired twice."

"How did you ascertain that?"

"I found the waddings of the pistol."

"And what became of the bullet which did not kill the horse?"

"It cut in two the feather of the hat belonging to him against whom it was directed, and broke a small birch at the other end of the open glade."

"In that case, then, the man on the black horse was disarmed, whilst his adversary had still one more shot to fire?"

"Sire, while the dismounted rider was extricating himself from his horse, the other was reloading his pistol. Only, he was much agitated while he was loading it, and his hand trembled greatly."

"How do you know that?"

"Half the charge fell to the ground, and he threw the ramrod aside, not having time to replace it in the pistol."

"Monsieur d'Artagnan, this is marvelous you tell me."

"It is only close observation, sire, and the commonest highwayman could tell as much."

"The whole scene is before me from the manner in which you relate it."

"I have, in fact, reconstructed it in my own mind, with merely a few alterations."

"And now," said the king, "let us return to the dismounted cavalier. You were saying that he walked towards his adversary while the latter was loading his pistol."

"Yes; but at the very moment he himself was taking aim, the other fired."

"Oh!" said the king; "and the shot?"

"The shot told terribly, sire; the dismounted cavalier fell upon his face, after having staggered forward three or four paces."

"Where was he hit?"

"In two places; in the first place, in his right hand, and then, by the same bullet, his chest."

"But how could you ascertain that?" inquired the king, full of admiration.

"By a very simple means; the butt end of the pistol was covered with blood, and the trace of the bullet could be observed, with fragments of a broken ring. The wounded man, in all probability, had the ring-finger and the little finger carried off."

"As far as the hand goes, I have nothing to say; but the chest?"

"Sire, there were two small pools of blood, at a distance of about two feet and a half from each other. At one of these pools of blood the grass was torn up by the clenched hand; at the other, the grass was simply pressed down by the weight of the body."

"Poor De Guiche!" exclaimed the king.

"Ah! it was M. de Guiche, then?" said the musketeer, quietly. "I suspected it, but did not venture to mention it to your majesty."

"And what made you suspect it?"

"I recognised the De Grammont arms upon the holsters of the dead horse."

"And you think he is seriously wounded?"

"Very seriously; since he fell immediately, and remained a long time in the same place; however, he was able to walk, as he left the spot, supported by two friends."

"You met him returning, then?"

"No; but I observed the footprints of three men; the one on the right and the one on the left walked freely and easily, but the one in the middle dragged his feet as he walked; besides, he left traces of blood at every step he took."

"Now, monsieur, since you saw the combat so distinctly that not a single detail seems to have escaped you, tell me something about De Guiche's adversary."

"Oh, sire, I do not know him."

"And yet you see everything very clearly."

"Yes, sire, I see everything; but I do not tell all I see; and, since the poor devil has escaped, your majesty will permit me to say that I do not intend to denounce him."[57]

The skilled tracker is aided by the lucky coincidence of a recent rainfall that permits the making of deductions bordering on omniscience—but the facts are, of course, obvious and speak for themselves. The protodetective also assumes the role of judge and refuses to identify the culprit to the court of justice. When the king compliments D'Artagnan as the cleverest man in his kingdom, the musketeer responds, "Oh, sire, a man may be mistaken; humanum est errare"—"In that case, you are not human, Monsieur d'Artagnan, for I believe you never are mistaken."

The opening pages of *The Three Musketeers* compared D'Artagnan to Don Quixote no less than six times:

—a Don Quixote of eighteen
—a Don Quixote without his corselet, without his coat of mail, without his cuistres
—a Don Quixote clothed in a woolen doublet
—the Don Quixote of this second Rosinate
—morally and physically, an exact copy of the hero of Cervantes
—Don Quixote took windmills for giants, and sheep for armies; D'Artagnan took every smile for an insult, and every look as a provocation

Years later, Dumas concludes the evolution of his wise-fool from youthful swashbuckler to Marshal of France in a manner to recall the concluding verse of Cervantes,

> . . . en tal coyuntura,
> Que acreditó su ventura,
> Morir cuerdo y vivir loco[58]
>
> he had the wisdom in his age
> to live a fool and die a sage.

THE METHOD OF ZADIG

> The Creator does not set out from a set of data, and proceed, like a crossword solver or a student of elementary algebra, to deduce from them a result which shall be final, predictable, complete and the only one possible.
> —Dorothy Sayers, *The Mind of the Maker*

> *Tu non pensavi ch'io löico fossi.*
> Thou didst not think that I was a logician.
> —Dante, *Inferno* 27

Voltaire's story "Zadig" (1747) gave rise to Huxley's reference to the "method of Zadig," in which unbiased observation and the indiscriminate collection of facts would automatically lead to correct deductions. With that sort of method one might expect Voltaire's protagonist to be a proto-Holmes, a cold thinking machine. But the text describes a young man with "nothing stiff or affected in his behavior" and one whose analytic style was quite flexible: "he did not pretend to examine every action by the strict rules of reason, but was always ready to make proper allowances for the weakness of mankind."

Zadig's deductive skills are almost exclusively those of the tracker. Arrested for being able to describe in detail the queen's lost dog and the king's missing horse while claiming ignorance of their whereabouts, he is found guilty of complicity in their theft. When the animals are later found, he is acquitted and allowed to explain his almost magical knowledge:

> "Ye stars of justice, abyss of sciences, mirrors of truth, who have the weight of lead, the hardness of iron, the splendor of the diamond, and many properties of gold: Since I am permitted to speak before this august assembly, I swear to you by Oramades that I have never seen the queen's respectable spaniel, nor the sacred horse of the king of kings. The truth of the matter was as follows: I was walking toward the little wood, where I afterwards met the venerable eunuch, and the most illustrious chief-huntsman. I observed on the sand the traces of an animal, and could easily perceive them to be those of a little dog. The light and long furrows impressed on little eminences of sand between the marks of the paws plainly discovered that it was a female, whose dugs were hanging down, and that therefore she must have whelped a few days before. Other traces of a different kind, that always appeared to have gently brushed the surface of the sand near the marks of the forefeet, showed me that she had very long ears; and as I remarked that there was always a slighter impression made on the sand by one foot than the other three, I found that the spaniel of our august queen was a little lame, if I may be allowed the expression.

"With regard to the horse of the king of kings, you will be pleased to know that, walking in the lanes of this wood, I observed the marks of a horse's shoes, all at equal distances. This must be a horse, said I to myself, that gallops excellently. The dust on the trees in the road that was but seven feet wide was a little brushed off, at a distance of three feet and a half from the middle of the road. This horse, said I, has a tail three feet and a half long, which being whisked to the right and left, has swept away the dust. I observed under the trees that formed an arbor five feet in height, that the leaves of the branches were newly fallen; from whence I inferred that the horse had touched them, and that he must therefore be five feet high. As to his bit, it must be gold of twenty-three carats, for he had rubbed its bosses against a stone which I knew to be a touchstone, and which I have tried. In a word, from the marks made by his shoes on flints of another kind, I concluded that he was shod with silver eleven deniers fine."[59]

Zadig is naïve and innocent, a child hero in a fairy tale. The moral of his story is that it can be dangerous to know too much. Zadig later refuses to use his observational skills to locate an escaped criminal; his philosophy of noninvolvement is that of his creator: *nous faut cultiver notres jardins*.

BEYOND GOOD AND EVIL: DON QUIXOTE AND THE STUDY OF MEDICINE

>Watson: You're just like Don Quixote; everything is always something else.
>Justin: He had a point; he went a bit too far, that's all. He thought that every windmill was a giant. That's insane. But thinking that they might be—
>—Goldman, *They Might Be Giants*

>He is the consort of the Queen of Fact
>—Wallace Stevens

Physicians have often been mistakenly advised to read the Sherlock Holmes stories for their brilliant examples of clinical deductive reasoning. It is perhaps more than coincidental that one of the greatest physicians of all time, Thomas Sydenham, recommended Cervantes to the boorish Sir Richard Blackmore—"when one Day I asked him to advise me what Books I should read to qualify me for Practice, he replied, Read *Don Quixot*, it is a very good Book, I read it still."[60] John Locke interpreted the importance of this advice in that it exhibited a respect for experience over theory. The true value of both Sherlock Holmes and Don Quixote for the physician is their dramatic representation of a vast cross-section of human personalities and motivations set against the frequently confusing contrast between appearance and reality. One of the morals to both series of tales seems to be that a passionate commitment to justice may facilitate the perception of reality.

Both Miguel de Cervantes Saavedra and Arthur Conan Doyle were sons of incompetent fathers. In all of Cervantes's works filial love is absent, and the chirurgeon (Cervantes's father was a barber surgeon) is always referred to by the perjorative epithet *"sacapotros,"* "boil splitter," with respect being reserved for licensed ("real") doctors. The trauma of Doyle's failed alcoholic father had a similar far-reaching influence on his detective fiction, a theme that has been carefully dissected by Freudian critics of his work. Against this background of a strained (at the very least) father-son relationship, the relationship between Doyle and Sherlock Holmes is in many ways quite analogous to the relationship between Cervantes and Don Quixote and indeed may be the identical relationship—failed father (author): successful son (created character). Their literary creations outshone the flesh-and-blood authors; in Cervantes's words, "every man is the son of his own works" (1.4).[61] The minor works of the creators of Don Quixote and Sherlock Holmes would not be the subjects of critical scholarship or other notice in the absence of their immortal heroes. Their other literary achievements would barely rate an obscure bibliographic footnote in a doubly obscure pedantic monograph.

Outlining the saga of Sherlock Holmes utilizing some passages from Don Quixote is perhaps the easiest way of suggesting the striking thematic similarities between these epics separated by three centuries. With his deerstalker cap, Inverness cape, meerschaum pipe, and magnifying glass, Holmes certainly presents "the strangest and most ridiculous figure imaginable" (1.2). The great detective and his "squire" Watson are candidates for "the most extraordinary couple the world had ever yet produced" (2.7). "The knight and the squire seem both to be cast in the same mould, and the madness of the one without the folly of the other would not be worth a rush" (2.2). Holmes sets himself up as the first representative of a new profession, that of consulting detective: "I am a novel knight in the world, and the first to resuscitate the now forgotten exercise of adventurous knighthood" (P1.47.109). Holmes is not the representative of cold deductive logic and sterile inhuman reason; that role is reserved for the official police (and the Bachelor Samson Carrasco). His major concern is justice: "I was born into the world to right such wrongs" (1.52); "we are Heaven's ministers upon earth, and the arms by which God executes His justice" (1.13); "I was born in this age of iron to revive in it that of gold" (1.20). In the words of Navarro Ledesma, "reason and truth are the real knight-errantry: reason and truth which wander helpless through the world, beaten here, stoned there, unrecognized by the foolish, persecuted by the mediocre, poorly rewarded and treated ungratefully by all the world."[62]

Modern scientific advances used by criminals (and wizards) require an updating of police techniques: "Perhaps the chivalry and enchantment of our time must follow a different road than they used to" (P1.47.70). The official police continually accept appearances at face value, "for all persons have not the sense to see things in the right point of view" (1.21). Holmes's method is to "guess at the clue by the thread" (1.4). He frequently begins a new adventure by deducing the identity of his client from obscure observations: "by the signs and samples of your clothes . . . I understand that you have had a miraculous liberation" (P1.41.73)—a trick that can be mistaken for mind reading: "in short observe all her activities and motions . . . if you recount them to me as they occurred, I will be able to infer what she keeps hidden in her innermost heart" (P2.10.74)—and impresses his gullible companion: "yet I think the credulity of the squire still more extraordinary" (2.2). Every objective appearance can be deceptive, "unless it be a clue to solve the mystery" (P1.23.73). (To what extent was Moriarity—the greatest of the windmills of the plain—a paranoid delusion?) Observation is supported by an extensive library of crime history (popular literature); presented with an unusual clue Holmes will have "recourse to his usual remedy, which was to recollect some incident in his books" (1.5). If necessary, Holmes will get down on all fours to make close physical contact with the material facts of the case: "but now I say that it is necessary to touch appearances with one's hand to be disabused" (P2.11.34).

Sherlock's Dulcinea, his *princesse lointaine,* is Irene Adler, and his often misunderstood and misinterpreted respect for her is a classic example of the medieval ethos of courtly love: "I have satisfied wrongs, righted injustices, punished insolence, conquered giants, and trampled monsters underfoot; I am in love, but only because knights must be in love; and being so, I am not of the licentious kind but of those who are restrained and platonic" (P2.32.105). The requirement that the *midons*, the lady of the Provençal poet, be married (to another) is satisfied before the end of "A Scandal in Bohemia." When Osler recommended that the young physician put his emotions on ice, to avoid Amaryllis in the shade, to beware the tangles of Neaera's hair, he was certainly not advising a rejection of sexuality that would prevent moral and emotional maturity. Dante's dedication to Beatrice as *the* woman in his life did not exclude marriage, children, and a total commitment to his craft.

The adventures of Holmes and Watson (Don Quixote and Sancho

Panza) are recounted in a loosely connected string of sorties; they repeatedly leave and then return home—all to the consternation of the likes of Mrs. Hudson, Mrs. Watson, and Mrs. Theresa Panza. The characters of Cervantes and Doyle discuss and allude to a large variety of literature of all types (but especially "popular") and openly express concern for their own literary personas, the public image of their important mission. There are fraudulent ("rediscovered," "recently uncovered") adventures (Alonso Fernandez de Avellanda was the earliest such theft in an age when coypright had no meaning) to further supplement the never published original written sources— Watson's notes, Cid Hamet Benengeli's chronicle. (Unamuno suggested that this fictitious Arab historican was not a pure literary device, but rather encompassed the profound truth "that the history was dictated to Cervantes by another man, whom Cervantes harbored within himself, a spirit who dwelt in the depths of his soul."63)

With a major division of the adventures of both hero pairs into two parts, some critics have considered the later series suspect, inferior or otherwise qualitatively different, while the majority of readers continue to regard them as integral to the sagas and genuine. When Cervantes and Doyle found it necessary to kill off their protagonists— "what have you to answer for in robbing the world of so diverting a madman?" (2.65)—neither succeeded—"there can never be too much of what is really good" (1.24)—and the resulting endless series of commentaries, criticisms, continuations, biographies, forgeries, and slanders have testified to the existential vitality of their creations. Mortal fathers had generated immortal sons.

HAMLET'S MILL

> Murder is alwaies reveled; the Goddes suffreth no vice unpunished.
> —William Adlington

> That rarest of gifts, a perfectly balanced mind
> —Lewis Carroll

> The mystery itself had to do with Eros gone awry.
> —Nora Gallagher, *Simple Pleasures*

John Gielgud's 1964 production of *Hamlet* yielded a Prince of Denmark who was cold, ironic, and supremely intelligent. While more than adequately depicting one of Shakespeare's most complex characters, Richard Burton scrupulously avoided the romantic sentimentality usually employed to indicate the tragedy of conflicting loyalties. More than any other interpretation, Burton's Hamlet clearly exhibited that passion of intellect belonging to the detective hero trying to solve a murder.[64] At first sight, the similarities between Shakespeare's hero and Sherlock Holmes seem superficial and slight: the solution of a murder, an aversion to women, a flair for the dramatic, a love of theater, a denial of the supernatural, and an intense mood lability. Yet there was something in Burton's performance (and in Shakespeare's text) that suggests a deeper affinity.

In the third book of his *Gesta Danorum*, Saxo Grammaticus (1150–1216) narrates the tale of Amlethus, son of Orvendel. King Orvendel of Denmark, "brightest of angels sent to men on middle-earth," is killed by his jealous brother Fengo; "then he took the wife of the brother he had butchered, capping unnatural murder with incest." Saxo then chronicles Amleth's use of guile to avenge his father's murder:

> Amleth beheld all this, but feared lest too shrewd a behaviour might make his uncle suspect him. So he chose to feign dullness, and pretend an utter lack of wits. This cunning course not only concealed his intelligence, but ensured his safety. Every day he remained in his mother's house utterly listless and unclean, flinging himself on the ground and bespattering his person with foul and filthy dirt. His discoloured face and visage smutched with slime denoted foolish and grotesque madness. All he said was of a piece with these follies; all he did savoured of utter lethargy. . . .
>
> He used at times to sit over the fire, and, raking up the embers with his hands, to fashion wooden crooks, and harden them in the fire, shaping at their tips certain barbs, to make them hold more tightly to their fastenings. When asked what he was about, he said that he was preparing sharp javelins to avenge his father. This answer was not a little scoffed at, all men deriding his idle and ridiculous pursuit; but the thing helped his purpose afterwards. Now it was his craft in this matter that first awakened in the deeper observers a suspicion of his cunning. For his skill in a trifling art betokened the hidden talent of a craftsman. . . . Lastly, he always watched with the most punctual care over his pile of stakes that he had pointed in the fire. Some people, therefore, declared that his mind was quick enough, and fancied that he only played the simpleton . . .
>
> When they averred that he had given a cunning answer, he answered that he had spoken deliberately: for he was loth to be thought prone to lying about any matter, and wished to be held a stranger to falsehood; and accordingly he mingled craft and candour in such wise that, though his words did lack truth, yet there was nothing to betoken the truth and betray how far his keenness went.
>
> But a friend of Fengo, gifted more with assurance than judgement, declared that the unfathomable cunning of such a mind could not be detected by a vulgar plot, for the man's obstinacy was so great that it ought not to be assailed with any mild measures. . . . Accordingly, said he, his

own profounder acuteness had hit on a more delicate way, which was well fitted to be put in practice, and would effectually discover what they desired to know. Fengo was purposely to absent himself, pretending affairs of great import. Amleth should be closeted alone with his mother in her chamber; but a man should first be commissioned to place himself in a concealed part of the room and listen heedfully to what they talked about. . . . The speaker, loth to seem readier to devise than to carry out the plot, zealously proffered himself as the agent of the eavesdropping. Fengo rejoiced of the scheme, and departed on pretence of a long journey. Now he who had given this counsel repaired privily to the room where Amleth was shut up with his mother, and lay down skulking in the straw. But Amleth had his antidote for the treachery.

Afraid of being overheard by some eavesdropper, he at first resorted to his usual imbecile ways, and crowed like a noisy cock, beating his arms together to mimic the flapping of wings. Then he mounted the straw and began to swing his body and jump again and again, wishing to try if aught lurked there in hiding. Feeling a lump beneath his feet, he drove his sword into the spot, and impaled him who lay hid. Then he dragged him from his concealment and slew him. Then, cutting his body into morsels, he seethed it in boiling water, and flung it through the mouth of an open sewer for the swine to eat, bestrewing the stinking mire with his hapless limbs. Having in this wise eluded the snare, he went back to the room. Then his mother set up a great wailing and began to lament her son's folly to his face but he said: "Most infamous of women! dost thou seek with such lying lamentations to hide thy most heavy guilt? Wantoning like a harlot, thou has entered a wicked and abominable state of wedlock, embracing with incestuous bosom thy husband's slayer. . . ." With such reproaches he rent the heart of his mother and redeemed her to walk in the ways of virtue.

When Fengo returned, nowhere could he find the man who had suggested the treacherous espial . . . Amleth, among others, was asked in jest if he had come on any trace of him, and replied that the man had gone to the sewer, but had fallen through its bottom and been stifled by the floods of filth, and that he had then been devoured by the swine that came up all about that place. This speech was flouted by those who heard; for it seemed senseless, though really it expressly avowed the truth.

Fengo now suspected that his stepson was certainly full of guile, and desired to make away with him, but durst not do the deed for fear of the displeasure, not only of Amleth's grandsire Rorik, but also of his own wife. So he thought that the King of Britain should be employed to slay him, so that another could do the deed, and he be able to feign innocence . . .

It is during his trip to England that Amleth's deductive skills are exhibited. Cunning and wisdom come from the mouth of a seeming fool: the meaning of the name Amleth is "simpleton," "stupid," "like unto a dumb animal."

Two retainers of Fengo then accompanied him, bearing a letter graven in wood . . . this letter enjoined the King of the Britons to put to death the youth who was sent over to him. While they were reposing, Amleth searched their coffers, found the letter, and read the instructions therein. Whereupon he erased all the writing on the surface, substituted fresh characters, and so, changing the purport of the instructions, shifted his own doom upon his companions. Nor was he satisfied with removing from himself the sentence of death and passing the peril on to others, but added an entreaty that the King of Britain would grant his daughter in marriage to a youth of great judgement whom he was sending to him. Under this was falsely marked the signature of Fengo.

Now when they had reached Britain, the envoys went to the king and proffered him the letter which they supposed was an implement of destruction to another, but which really betokened death to themselves. The king dissembled the truth, and entreated them hospitably and kindly. Then Amleth scouted all the splendour of the royal banquet like vulgar viands, and abstaining very strangely, rejected that plenteous feast, refraining from the drink even as from the banquet. All marvelled that a youth and a forcigner should disdain the carefully cooked dainties of the royal board and the luxurious banquet provided, as if it were some peasant's relish. So, when the revel broke up, and the king was dismissing his friends to rest, he had a man sent into the sleeping room to listen secretly, in order that he might hear the midnight conversation of his guests. Now, when Amleth's companions asked him why he had refrained from the feast of yestereve, as if it were poison, he answered that the bread was flecked with blood and tainted; that there was a tang of iron in the liquor; while the meats of the feast reeked the stench of a human carcase, and were infected by a kind of smack of the odour of the charnel. He further said that the king had the eyes of a slave, and that the queen had in three ways shown the behaviour of a bondmaid. Thus he reviled with insulting invective not so much the feast as its givers. And presently his companions, taunting him with his old defect of wits, began to flout him with many saucy jeers. . . .

All this the king heard from his retainer; and declared that he who could say such things had either more than mortal wisdom or more than mortal folly. . . . Then he summoned his steward and asked him whence he had procured the bread. . . . The king asked where the corn had grown of which it was made, and whether any sign was to be found there of human carnage? The other answered, that not far off was a field, covered with the ancient bones of slaughtered men, and still bearing plainly all the signs of ancient carnage. . . . The king . . . took the pains to learn also what had been the source of the lard. The other declared that his hogs had, through negligence, strayed from keeping, and battened on the rotten carcase of a robber, and that perchance their pork had thus come to have something of a corrupt smack. The king, finding that Amleth's judgement was right in this thing also, asked of what liquor the steward had mixed the drink? Hearing that it had been brewed of water and meal, he had the spot of the spring pointed out to him, and set to digging deep down; and there he found rusted away, several swords, the tang whereof it was thought had tainted the waters. Others relate that Amleth blamed the drink because, while quaffing it, he had detected some bees that had fed in the paunch of a dead man; and that the taint, which had formerly been imparted to the combs, had reappeared in the taste. The king . . . had a secret interview with his mother, and asked her who his father had really been. She said she had submitted to no man but the king. But when he threatened that he would have the truth out of her by a trial, he was told that he was the offspring of a slave. . . . Abashed as he was with shame for his low estate, he was so ravished with the young man's cleverness that he asked him why he had aspersed the queen with the reproach that she had demeaned herself like a slave? But while resenting that the courtliness of his wife had been accused in the midnight gossip of a guest, he found that her mother had been a bondmaid. . . . Then the king adored the wisdom of Amleth as though it were inspired. . . .

After demonstrating such sharp observational skills, Amleth's return to Denmark is somewhat disappointing. His homecoming is marked by his own funeral rites, and he pricks his finger on his sword, but the rest is just another crude revenge plot. This proto-Hamlet successfully regains his throne, but later refinements never again allow him as much careful deliberation and cunning intelligence as Saxo's primitive version.

O valiant Amleth, and worthy of immortal fame, who being shrewdly armed with a feint of folly, covered a wisdom too high for human wit under a marvellous disguise of silliness! and not only found in his subtlety means to protect his own safety, but also by its guidance found opportunity to avenge his father. By this skillful defence of himself, and strenuous revenge for his parent, he has left it doubtful whether we are to think more of his wit or his bravery.[65]

THE THREE PRINCES AND THE EASTERN ORIGIN OF SERENDIPITY

> There are no accidents either; we attract events and color them.
> —Dahlberg, *Confessions*

> If you do not expect the unexpected, you will not find it.
> —Heraclitus

Voltaire derived his concept of Zadig from Thomas Simon Gueulette's *Soirées Bretonnes* (1712), a French translation of a sixteenth-century Italian text, *Peregrinaggio di tre giovani, figliuli del re di Serendippo; tradotto dalla lingua persiana in lingua italiana da M. Christoforo Armenio* (Travels of the Three Young Sons of the King of Serendip, Translated from the Persian Language into Italian by Christopher the Armenian). The Persian original is uncertain, but it has been variously identified as *Hasht Bihist* (Eight Paradises) collected by the Persian poet Amir Khusrau (1253–1325), Nizami's *Seven Beauties*, or *Nigarstan* (The Picture Gallery, 1335), a miscellany of stories and poetry by Muin-al-din Juraini.[66] It is now fairly certain that Christopher the Armenian is a fiction. When Michele Tramezzino published the *Peregrinaggio* in 1557, he was himself retelling (not translating) tales orally current along the great Renaissance sea routes.

A later French translation by Le Chevalier de Mailly, *Le voyage et les aventures des trois princes de Sarendip* (1721), was read by the young Horace Walpole as a child and he recalled it later in life when he was looking for a word to suggest a certain type of accidental sagacity. In a letter to Horace Mann in 1754, Walpole described the origin of his neologism, serendipity: "I once read a silly fairy tale, called *The Three Princes of Serendip:* as their highnesses travelled, they were always making discoveries, by accidents and sagacity, of things which they were not in quest of: for instance, one of them discovered that a mule blind of the right eye had travelled the same road lately, because the grass was eaten only on the left side, where it was worse than on the right."[67] Most of the young men's deductions fall into the realm of the tracker: lameness is predicted from one footprint dragging, and loads of butter and honey are indicated by the ants and flies along the trail. By similar thought processes, the princes infer that one of his counselors plans to kill the Emperor Beramo. Since the traitor cannot be punished unless the crime be proven—"So that for lack of his own confession, I can never rightly convict him"— the young men devise a stratagem to entrap the culprit who eventually confesses and is pardoned. Later in the *Peregrinaggio* the emperor learns how to transform himself so that he can go among his vassals in disguise, uncover their inner thoughts, and punish the wicked and reward the good. The three princes treat their early amazing deductions from scant evidence with a certain levity: the details they focus upon happen to coincide with the truth. But their later adventures involve them in the outwitting of criminals and the prevention of murder. Faced with these challenges, the young men exhibit none of Zadig's temerity.

"You must observe," cautioned Walpole, "that no discovery of a thing you *are* looking for comes under this description." Serendipity involves looking for one thing and finding another. It is a "particular kind of natural cleverness," a gift or a knack, but not an act. *Sortes Walpolianae* (Walpole's luck) was one of the phenomena covered by the term: Horace's uncanny ability to find what he needed when he wasn't looking for it, a personal magnetism to attract coincidence. It is the converse of the schlimazl's (bad luck) fate with his penchant for lucklessness. Dr. James Austin has attempted to chart those personality traits that attract good luck and facilitate discovery and invention (table 2). Artistic creativity, scientific breakthroughs, the ability to select research problems capable of solution or mysteries amenable to detection are all expressions of serendipity.

Deductive reasoning applies general propositions or universal truths to particular facts or concrete instances; induction reverses the direction of the inference by collecting a sufficient number of particular instances to support a general hypothesis. "Why," asked Mill, "is a single instance, in some cases, sufficient for a complete induction, while, in others, myriads of concurring instances, without a single exception known or presumed, go such a very little way toward establishing a universal proposition?"[69] Children engage in an inaccurate but sometimes correct reasoning from particular to particular, a process referred to as transduction. The American philosopher Charles Saunders Peirce (1839–1914) used the terms *abduction* and *retroduction* to describe the process by which the human mind could go from admittedly insufficient particulars to a correct generalization; a more popular term for this instinctive reasoning is *guessing*.[70] The study of insight and intuition in science needs to take greater account of the position of abduction/retroduction halfway between transduction and induction/deduction. Creativity seems rooted in part in the ability to retain childhood's sense of wonder.

THE ROYAL HUNT OF THE SON

"The Game's afoot"
—Shakespeare *Henry IV, Part 1*

Indagator sagax et indefessus
—William Cole

Man hunting is the avocation fitted for heroes.
—James Payn, *Lost Sir Massingberd*

Our god is a hunter
—Euripides, *Bacchantes*

Table 2
Kinds of Good Luck[68]

Type	Elements Involved	Personality Traits Needed
Chance I	"Blind" luck	None
Chance II	Kettering Principle: "I have never heard of anyone stumbling on something sitting down." Chance favors those in motion; events are brought together to form "happy accidents" when you diffusely apply your energies in motions that are typically nonspecific.	Curiosity about many things, persistence, willingness to experiment and to explore.
Chance III	Pasteur Principle: "*le hazard ne favorise que les esprits préparés.*" Chance favors the prepared mind. Some special receptivity born from past experience permits you to discern a new fact or to perceive ideas in a new relationship.	A background of knowledge, based on your abilities to observe, remember, and quickly form significant new associations.
Chance IV	Disraeli Principle: "we make our fortunes, and we call them fate." Chance favors the individualized action. Fortuitous events occur when you behave in ways that are highly distinctive of you as a person.	Distinctive hobbies, personal life-styles, and activities peculiar to you, as an individual, especially when they operate in domains seemingly far removed from the area of the discovery.
Chance I–IV	Fleming Effect: The most novel, if not the greatest discoveries, occur when several varieties of chance coincide. (This must be distinguished from what Kingsley Amis refers to as the Fleming effect, an imaginative use of information. This literary characteristic might just as well be called the Doyle effect or the Stevenson effect.)	All of the above.

Hunting is the oldest occupation. In the third book of *The Mythologies*, Fulgentius associates Perdix (the partridge) with the Paleolithic rejection of the nomadic for the agricultural life: bored with "the bloody destruction involved in the slaughter of wild animals and the loneliness of the roving chase" he turns to wearisome labor and invention. A legendary hunter, nephew and apprentice to Daedalus, Perdix invented the chisel, the saw, the potter's wheel, and the compass. He was killed by his mentor and uncle partly out of jealousy and partly because he was suspected of an incestuous relationship with his mother. Bloody destruction for the hunted, bloody destruction for the hunter.[71]

The riddle of the Sphinx is a hunter's riddle. The Sphinx herself is a composite beast, several prey in one—a hunter's dream. And for the detective, Cocteau's Sphinx is described as "the most mysterious criminal of our time."[72] A tracker would have no difficulty answering the Sphinx's query: "What creature walks on four legs in the morning, two legs at noon and three legs in the evening?" Especially when the man-hunter himself limped and was familiar with his own unique tracks. By solving this riddle and later discovering his own patricide, Oedipus ("swell-foot") on both occasions saves many lives but earns general acclaim for the first deed and universal opprobrium for the latter. Recall that Fulgentius's prototypical hunter was also implicated in incest.

In his preface to *The Millionairess*, Bernard Shaw categorized hunting as both horrible in itself and socially dangerous because "it revives a primitive instinct incompatible with civilization: indeed civilization rests fundamentally on the compact that it shall be dropped."[73] The theme of the hunt is frequently alluded to in Doyle's detective fiction and in all murder mysteries. Poe's "the scent had never for an instant been lost," D'Artagnan's, Zadig's, and the three princes of Serendip's tracking skills nevertheless suggest that the nomadic thrill of the hunt may reflect something deeper than primitive blood-lust and that the ultimate hunt—the manhunt—may be an image open to an alternative meaning.

In his philosophical essay on the nature of hunting, the Spanish philosopher Ortega y Gasset points out that hunting cannot be defined by either its purpose or its techniques. Hunting is not exclusively utilitarian (the obtaining of food) or sporting (a useless diversion). Not only is hunting not defined by techniques but progress in weaponry is foreign to its very essence. Hunting cannot substantially progress: "as the weapon became more and more effective, man imposed more and more limitations on himself . . . in order to avoid making the prey and the hunter excessively unequal."[74] Hunting excludes equality, is not reciprocal; it is "what an animal does to take possession, dead or alive, of some other being that belongs to a species basically inferior to its own. Vice versa, if there is to be a hunt, this superiority of the hunter over the prey cannot be absolute."[75] Hunting occurs on the level of instinct, not that of reason. Although reason is one of the techniques that the hunter may use, hunting is essentially "a contest or confrontation between two systems of instincts."[76] At the human level, the instinctual choice of values, good or evil, colors the organism's whole manner of behavior so that the criminal while using the same rational techniques as the detective is, nevertheless, of an inferior species than the detective/hunter. A major part of the difficulty of hunting results from a presumed scarcity of game—game worthy of the hunt. How often does Holmes complain of boredom because of a lack of interesting crimes. "The hunt is a series of technical operations, and for an activity to become technical it has to matter that it works in one particular way and not in another. Technique presupposes that success in reaching a certain goal is difficult and improbable; to compensate for its difficulty and improbability one must exert oneself to invent a special procedure of sufficient effectiveness."[77] The necessity for the detective to utilize the latest in scientific technology is dictated by the criminal's use of the same.

The hunter adheres to his own strict code of ethics. His natural element is solitude and his life style is monastic in its artificial limitations. The principal technique employed by the hunter involves imitating the hunted. "In that mystical union with the beast a contagion is immediately generated and the hunter begins to behave like the game."[78] When the game is animal, the hunter deliberately steps back into the animal in his nature. When the game is human, the hunter uses his creative imagination to predict the moves of his criminal prey. The venatic art remains an art and does not become a science. The goal of a science of hunting would be power, control, total victory, the eradication of all game, the end of the precarious ecological balance between the hunter and the hunted, the end of the game.

5
The General Theory of Detection: Sense and Non-Sense in Science

> HENRY. Good God, woman, face the facts.
> ELEANOR. Which ones? We've got so many.
> —Goldman, *The Lion in Winter*

> Simple facts in isolation, and facts to connect them—ands and buts—are the *sine qua non* of all their glorious achievement. But there are no such facts. Connectedness is the essence of everything. —John Gardner, *Grendel*

> Against that positivism which stops before phenomena, saying "there are only *facts*," I should say: no, it is precisely facts that do not exist, only *interpretations*.
> —Nietzsche

> Facts are ventriloquists' dummies.
> —Aldous Huxley

> The sense of the world must lie outside the world.
> —Wittgenstein, *Tractatus Logico-Philosophicus*

THE MYTH OF SCIENCE IN THE NINETEENTH CENTURY: THE DOGMA OF THE IMMACULATE PERCEPTION

> Our steps must be guided by a clue.
> —Francis Bacon

Francis Bacon authored the classic version of the Renaissance allegation that the ancient world and the Middle Ages had relied too exclusively on religious dogma and abstract deduction while they avoided reading at firsthand of the book of life. "Now what the sciences stand in need of is a form of induction which shall analyse experience and take it to pieces, and by a due process of exclusion and rejection lead to an inevitable conclusion."[79] The observation of myriads of facts, the classification of the resulting data, and the automatic elimination of untenable hypotheses were the mechanisms that Bacon offered to usher in the scientific utopia of the future: "I have provided the machine, but the stuff must be gathered from the facts of nature."[80]

The great astronomer Tycho Brahe (1546–1601) collected enormous masses of detailed observations on the movements of the heavenly bodies; his mind being free of any bias, his name is known to few today. His student Kepler (1571–1630) started with certain a priori theological assumptions about the nature of God the Creator, imagined an analogy between this God and his creation, and mathematically applied this analogy successfully to Tycho's data. The great discoveries in science owe little to the Baconian method; to ponder carefully and attempt to apply true Baconian principles will almost certainly condemn the student to a life of scientific achievement equal in sterility to Bacon's—the lord chancellor never successfully applied his method to yield any discovery of note. Another nonproductive philosopher of science, Herbert Spencer (1820–1903), would later repeat this fallacy of automatic induction: facts accumulated in his mind until they had arranged themselves neatly into a generalization. He was never bothered by lacunae in the data or discrepant facts: "I am never puzzled."[81]

In his *Back to Methuselah*, Shaw identified this lack of puzzlement as the secret of Darwin's popularity: "He never puzzled anybody. If very few of us have read the Origin of Species from end to end, it is not because it overtaxes our mind, but because we take in the whole case and are prepared to accept it long before we have come to the end of the innumerable instances and illustrations of which the book mainly consists. Darwin becomes tedious in the manner of a man who insists on continuing to prove his innocence after he has been acquitted. . . . he will have you listen to all the evidence that exists in the world. Darwin's industry was enormous. His patience, his perseverance, his conscientiousness reached the human limit. But he never got deeper beneath or higher above the facts than an ordinary man could follow him."[82]

The reality of scientific progress would have gradually reduced Bacon's position from one of prophet of the scientific method to one of quaint seventeenth-century essayist (his idols of the human mind were part of the general climate of ideas of that time) were it not that several famous scientists were themselves of such limited culture and philosophy that when asked how they arrived at their breakthroughs, they could only stammer forth their elementary catechism of the scientific method simplified. "I worked on true Baconian principles," wrote Charles Darwin, "and without any theory, collected facts on a wholesale scale. . . . After five years' work I allowed myself to speculate on the subject and drew up some short notes."[83] How often this absurd passage has been requoted to warp the minds of young students and inculcate an unrealistic vision of the true way of a scientific investigator. For more than a quarter century after the voyage of HMS *Beagle*, Darwin patiently amassed data; he was pressured to rush into print only by Wallace's impending publication of an identical theory. "Certainly no one who began so cautiously with facts ever got quite so deeply involved in ideas as Charles Darwin," wrote Irvine: "He gravely eschewed speculation, and speculation enveloped him"[84] The accepted spiritual itinerary of the Galapagos pilgrim from religious orthodoxy through indiscriminate fact collection, to the theory of natural selection and finally to an agnostic materialism is revealed in Darwin's early notebooks to be somewhat inaccurate. A materialist position shattered the religious orthodoxy first; the evolutionary hypothesis was then postulated as more consistent with his new philosophy of life, and finally came the decades of nuts-and-bolts work, critically arranging evidence to support a predetermined position. Long before he ever set to sea, Darwin had concluded (1) that God did not exist, (2) therefore, special creation of individual species, as currently accepted, was impossible, and (3) some other method of speciation—perhaps akin to grandfather Erasmus's "evolution"—must account for the countless stable differences between organisms.[85] Malthus would later provide Darwin's theory with its questionable motive force while Lyell would give the incomplete theory almost infinite expanses of time to cloak deficiencies that could not begin to be remedied until the development of modern genetics. Perhaps the truest element in his Victorian hagiography was Darwin's irrational fear of martyrdom. His persecution complex was quite justified: he recognized that the impetus and guiding idea for his theory was a heterodox theological construct.

The plodding Darwin admitted that much "fact-grinding" had destroyed his imaginative faculty and made him "nauseate Shakespeare": "My mind seems to have become a kind of machine for grinding general laws out of large collections of facts, but why this should have caused the atrophy of that part of the brain alone, on which the higher tastes depend, I cannot conceive. . . . The loss of these tastes is a loss of happiness, and may possibly be injurious to the intellect, and more probably to the moral character, by enfeebling the emotional part of our nature."[86] A misanthrope who was extremely pessimistic about the future benefits of science, H. G. Wells supported this distorted view of the great scientist: "nothing destroys the powers of general observation quite so much as a life of experimental science."[87] There is certainly an element of meticulousness in science; sloppiness is not tolerable. But it is just that component for which one designs robots or hires technicians. The creative thinker may very well be the one who always drops the test tube—the clumsy, absent-minded professor.

Collect facts at random—pluck a million chicken feathers—do they spontaneously organize themselves into the awesome and beautiful edifice that Darwin constructed? Wallace succeeded with only a fraction of Darwin's plodding patience—"Ten specimens are too many for a scientist." Facts have no existence by themselves but only within a schema. An isolated perception or cognition is an atomist's fantasy— the dogma of the immaculate perception. It is precisely facts that do not exist, only interpretations. Pattern and meaning emerge, not through the passive accumulation of endless details, but rather through the actively creating human imagination. Theories are overthrown by better theories, never merely by contradictory facts. The only true scientific facts are laws and generalizations; in Aristotle's terminology, science deals with universals, not with unique events.[88]

Nineteenth-century physics interpreted the interaction between atoms as a game of billiards and extended this perception to the universe. Thus, Pierre-Simon, marquis de Laplace (1749–1827), wrote in his *Essai philosophique sur les probabilités* (1820): "We ought then to regard the present state of the universe as the effect of its anterior state and as the cause of the one which is to follow. Given for one instant an intelligence which could comprehend all the forces by which nature is animated and the respective situation of the beings who compose it—an intelligence sufficiently vast to submit these data to analysis—it would embrace in the same formula the movements of the greatest bodies of the universe and those of the lightest atom; for it, nothing would be uncertain and the future, as the past, would be present to its eyes."[89] This philosophy was repeated by John Stuart Mill (1806–73) in his *A System of Logic* (1843): "The state of the whole universe at any instant we believe to be the consequence of its state at the previous instant; insomuch that one who knew all the agents which exist at the present moment, their collocation in space, and all their properties, in other words, the laws of their agency, could predict the whole subsequent history of the universe, at least unless some new volition of a power capable of controlling the universe should supervene."[90]

It follows that if a momentary onmiscience would make both the past and future clear to an observer then it should also be possible to deduce the entire universe from a single fact. Sherlock Holmes expressed this inverted logic in *A Study in Scarlet:* "From a drop of water, a logician could infer the possibility of an Atlantic or a Niagra without having seen or heard of one or the other. So all life is a great chain, the nature of which is known whenever we are shown a single link of it." And again in "The Five Orange Pips": "The ideal reasoner would, when he had once been shown a single fact in all its bearings, deduce from it not only all the chain of events which lead up to it but also all the results which could follow from it. As Cuvier could correctly describe a whole animal by the contemplation of a single bone, so the observer who has thoroughly understood one link in a series of incidents should be able to accurately state all the other ones, both before and after." Actually a single bone might be too much. Chirotherium left no fossil remains and was reconstructed from footprints.

The relationship between "Facts" and truth is not as easy to define as one might first imagine. First, any conceivable pattern can marshal an infinite number of facts to support it. Second, any set of observed facts will always fit more than one theory. And third, since any event can be made to appear inevitable from a variety of theories, predictability itself has only a limited role in any process of verification. The remark in the *Valley of Fear*—"And yet there should be no combination of events for which the wit of man cannot conceive an explanation"—can be interpreted as a reflection on a fundamental ambiguity inherent in the search for truth. The difficulties this presents in matters criminal are quite formidable and should lead logically to a Talmudic exclusion of all circumstantial evidence. Holmes was not insensitive to this problem—"Circumstantial evidence is a very tricky thing: it may seem to point very straight to one thing, but if you shift your own point of view a little, you may find it pointing in an equally uncompromising manner to something entirely different" ("Boscombe Valley Mystery")—and employed a number of dramatic traps to catch criminals in the act or elicit self-incriminating confessions.

IMAGINATION AND THE PSYCHOLOGY OF INVENTION

> But there is no intuition about it. It is mere observation.
> —August Derleth, *Adventures of Solar Pons*

> Observation is a theory-laden undertaking
> —N. R. Hanson, *Patterns of Discovery*

> Thinking is different from perceiving and is held to be in part imagination, in part judgement.
> —Aristotle, *De Anima*

> Thought can as it were *fly*, it doesn't have to walk.
> —Wittgenstein, *Zettel*

The nineteenth-century imposition of mechanistic determinism on psychology led Holmes to talk of moving ideas in and out of the lumber room of his compartmentalized brain; modern physics has inverted the process and now undertakes to apply organic and holistic images borrowed from the life sciences to its knowledge of the universe. Darwin testified that science destroyed imagination. The exact opposite—a necessary union between science and imagination—is a prerequisite for scientific progress. The act of discovery is not an inductive inference; it escapes logical analysis and defies psychological recipes. Genius, experience, and intuition combine with a certain random component that cannot be controlled but seems able to be attracted by serendipitous persons. "The mechanisms of discovery," Einstein told the poet Saint-John Perse, "are neither logical nor intellectual. It is a sudden illumination, almost a rapture. Later, to be sure, intelligence analyzes and experiments confirm (or invalidate) the intuition. But initially there is a great forward leap of the imagination."

The great French mathematician, Henri Poincaré, has left one of the most insightful records of the gestalt process of creation. He emphasized the absence of any routine mechanism for discovery: "In order to obtain a result having any real value it is not enough to grind out calculations, or to have a machine for putting things in order: it is not order only, but unexpected order, that has a value. A machine can take hold of the bare fact, but the soul of the fact will always escape it." For Poincaré it is the man and not the method that solves problems.[91]

The analogy that unites a cluster of disparate facts and leads to novel solutions is suggested by "the selected fact": "facts would be barren if there were not minds capable of selecting between them and distinguishing those which have something hidden behind them and recognizing what is hidden—minds which, behind the bare fact, can detect the soul of the fact."[92] After consciously but unsuccessfully struggling with a difficult question (stage of preparation), the problem solver "sleeps on it," thinks of something else *(penser à côté)*, or simply waits (stage of incubation/gestation) for insight or satori (stage of illumination). Unconscious work is performed by the subliminal ego, which is not purely automatic but is capable of discernment. The conscious mind recognizes the productive hypothesis by a "logical instinct that the truth must lie in a certain region," by an esthetic sense in tune with the realm of beauty, by the surprise of its simplicity. The logic of the verification process follows, but such logic is barren without the genius, intuition, synderesis, or illative sense that helps generate correct hunches. For Poincaré there was "nothing mysterious in the fact that every one is not capable of discovery.... intuition of mathematic order, which enables us to guess hidden harmonies and relations, cannot belong to every one."[93]

When Huxley, the "logic engine," recommended that one "sit down before the fact as a little child," he touched on one of the key insights of modern psychology. It is the retention into adulthood of certain characteristics of childhood cognition that seems to contribute most to creative thought (table 3). Inductive and deductive inferences, Pascal's esprit de geometrie, make sense only in a context of justification; discovery, insight, Pascal's esprit de finesse can only begin to make sense in the context of developmental psychology. Picturing a hypothetico-deductive model of the world is a game for children.

In the childhood of the world, when Galen held the ancient and

Table 3
Development of Selective Attention

The perceptual exploration of the child matures into the logical search of the adult, but the characteristics of the earlier stage are never completely renounced.[94]

Perceptual Exploration	*Logical Search*
impulsive	reflective
rapid	slow
shorter sequences	longer sequences
play	work
open-ended	well-specified goal
curiosity	goal-directed
divergent	convergent
controlled by salient/dominant/ reinforcement-correlated features of stimulus environment	controlled by task defined, informational needs, and logical constraints

medieval medical schools in thrall, a dissection was simply an occasionally accurate instance of a familiar text. Vesalius's anatomy injected an element of surprise into this previously sterile exercise. Nowadays medical students are expected to evidence the same heightened interest in a scientifically correct anatomy (the "familiar") accompanied by fairly limited submicroscopic increments (the "novel") as if these still captured the original excitement ("surprise") of the Renaissance age of discovery. This ignores the absence of any extrenched alternate expectations—an established Galenic or Ptolemaic dogmatic system.

Scientific texts are often written so as to make the creative leap appear obvious in retrospect; they continually depict the outdated theories of the past as plainly erroneous and the currently accepted scientific world view as patiently constructed and patently evident. The good guys are clearly discernible from the bad guys; truth and error are easily separated by p values. By confusing scientific progress with logical progression, this "high school" presentation of scientific development abandons to media such as detective fiction the dramatic protrayal of the greatest of human adventures: the Gestaltists' "aha-Erlebnis," the shock of recognition of a mismatch between expectation and actuality, the surprised perception of the significance of this discrepancy, the resultant focusing of attention, the sparking of curiosity and the sudden insight into a simpler and more profound unity of phenomena.

The closed universe of the detective story offers an extremely accurate psychological model of this process of scientific discovery and successfully communicates to the general public some of the complex interactions among data collection, insight and experience, hypothesis formation and verification. To cavil at the artificiality of a locked-room murder is to criticize the necessity for the researcher to control variables in the laboratory situation. In the broad human context of the criminal investigation, the murder mystery accurately reflects the excitement of a passionate commitment to truth.

The detective mystery can exist and flourish only in an age of science, but the truth of its vision lies more in the realm of human psychology than physico-chemical research. That is why, even apart from dead bodies, it has so much in common with the practice of medicine.

THE LEVELING TENDENCY

> There isn't a method that any fool can get hold of in order to do philosophy as we do it.
> —Richard Hare

> The intuitions of great men are sounder than the deductive demonstrations of mediocrities.
> —Morris Kline, *Mathematics*

> There are no methodologies which will enable mediocre men to produce the same results as great ones. Genius is not an infinite capacity for taking pains.
> —J. V. Langmead Casserley

Bacon's method has a strong democratic intention—a leveling tendency—in that it has no need of individual talent or genius. "For my way of discovering sciences goes far to level men's wits, and leaves but little to individual excellence; because it performs everything by the surest rules and demonstrations."[95] Mill questioned whether this "march of intellect be not rather a march towards doing without intellect, and supplying our deficiency of giants by the united efforts of a constantly increasing multitude of dwarfs?"[96] In this light, the computer may represent a revolutionary new tool or a *terminus ad quem* of the scientific mentality.

The science that is a collective or committee undertaking exults in anonymity or its equivalent, the identification of the ideal scientist with the intellectually commonplace. The system is everything, the individual nothing—"I am a very ordinary individual after all" (*A Study in Scarlet*). Such prosaic minds are diligent and scholarly; they cultivate the virtues of the worker bees. But they are also dry and dull, pedantic and plebian, literal and uninspired. Passionless and absent-minded drones like Dalton, Hooke, and Boyle may fit this Puritan myth, but biographies of mad magicians like Isaac Newton will need to be bowdlerized as unfit for modern youth.

One of the main functions of institutional science is to maintain or accentuate existing social inequalities. The nonvisionary scientist with his dependence on technique is a bureaucrat committed to expending public and private resources to maintain the system at all costs. Waste and ineptitude in science are defended with the same self-satisfied non-sequiturs utilized by nonscientific bureaucracies in pursuit of the identical goal—self-preservation. In the end, all bureaucracies take on the same facelessness, succeed at their primary goal (their own continued existence), and forget what they were created for. And when the New(er) Criticism writes a revolutionary article (and best-selling book) revealing that the emperor has no clothes on, it is feted by the system that long ago discovered that assimilation is a more successful tactic than retaliation.

Holmes often talks of the forensic science of the future as if the technology will be proof against the imbecilities of the official police.

He was assuming that their limitations were cognitive and not moral. The science of detection has gone beyond anything Holmes could have imagined and yet the relative percentage of unsolved murders has probably increased. A Gödel's Theorem of Criminology grounds this science in the nonscientific realm of good and evil, justice and mercy.

A BROWNIAN MOVEMENT: THE PLACE OF FACT IN A WORLD OF VALUE

> "Only a little murdered," he said, still smiling. "Yes, I think I should like some of them *rather* murdered. Not too much of course; its a question of a sense of proportion."
> —Chesterton, *Four Faultless Felons*

> I can believe the impossible, but not the improbable.
> —Chesterton, "The Curse of the Golden Cross"

> "I must not say who I am until the end of the world; but I may say what I am. I am the law."
> —Chesterton, *The Ball and the Cross*

Like Oliver Wendell Holmes, Gilbert Keith Chesterton was a master of two reprobate literary forms—the essay and the occasional poem. A prolific writer, he also made notable contributions in the areas of history, philosophy, theology, epic poetry, biography, autobiography, literary, artistic, and social criticism, the novel, the short story—and the detective story. Although Chesterton's master detective had a real-life prototype in Monsignor John O'Connor, he was conceived as a deliberate corrective to the popular (mis)interpretation of Sherlock Holmes. The contrast between the two detectives was physical as well as philosophical. Chesterton's commonplace and almost invisible prelate gave a poor impression of a perceptive detective: "Mr. Muggleton had read reports and romances about the Great Criminologist, who sits in his library like an intellectual spider, and throws out theoretical filaments of a web as large as the world. He was prepared to be led to the lonely chateau where the expert wore a purple dressing-gown, to the attick where he lived on opium and acrostics, to the vast laboratory or the lonely tower. To his astonishment he was led to the very edge of the crowded beach by the pier to meet a dumpy little clergyman, with a broad hat and a broad grin" ("The Pursuit of Mr. Blue").[97] Father Brown is one of those amateurs who always know more than the bumbling professionals: "The police have their faults, but thank God they're inefficient."[98] Drab, quiet, unostentatious, Brown seems closer to Watson than to Holmes. The priest and the physician have acquired experience of the human heart in situations marked by great stress and anxiety.

The Holmes canon is itself filled with an attitude of wonder at the ability of the simplest and smallest things to be clues to the deepest secrets. Although Holmes will refer to the use of chemical reagents, he will solve a case by the enigmatic clue of the curious failure of a dog to bark. He recognized that "there is nothing more deceptive than an obvious fact" ("The Boscombe Valley Mystery"). To Father Brown, plain literal facts have about them an element of the fantastic—"a kind of wild poetry of the commonplace"—that can actually obscure the truth: "the mere facts! Do you really admit—are you still so sunk in superstitions, so clinging to dim and prehistoric altars, that you believe in facts? . . . . the philosophy of this world may be founded on facts, its business is run on spiritual impressions and atmospheres." Facts can be quite deceptive—"Every detail points to something, certainly; but generally to the wrong thing. Facts point in all directions";[99] they allow alternate and contradictory interpretations—"ten false philosophies will fit the universe" ("The Honour of Israel Gow").[100] The facts that Father Brown considers important derive from an intuitive psychology of the criminal—identical to the psychology of the noncriminal: "All those things that 'aren't evidence' are what convince me. I think a moral impossibility the biggest of all impossibilities" ("The Strange Crime of John Boulnois").[101] If there is no unique criminal psychology, then there can be no science of criminology:

> Science is a grand thing when you can get it. . . . But what do these men mean, nine times out of ten, when they use it nowadays? When they say detection is a science? When they say criminology is a science? They mean getting *outside* a man and studying him as if he were a gigantic insect; in what they could call a dry impartial light; in what I should call a dead and dehumanized light. They mean getting a long way off him, as if he were a distant prehistoric monster; staring at the shape of his "criminal skull" as if it were a sort of eerie growth like the horn of a rhinoceros's nose. When the scientist talks about a type, he never means himself, but always his neighbour; probably his poorer neighbour. I don't deny the dry light may sometimes do good; though in one sense it's the very reverse of science. So far from being knowledge, it's actually suppression of what we know. It's treating a friend as a stranger, and pretending that something familiar is really remote and mysterious. It's like saying that a man has a proboscis between his eyes, or that he falls down in a fit of insensibility once every twenty-four hours. Well, what you call "the secret" is exactly the opposite. I don't try to get outside the man. I try to get inside the

murderer.... Indeed it's much more than that, don't you see? I *am* inside a man. I am always inside a man, moving his arms and legs; but I wait till I know I am inside a murderer, thinking his thoughts, wrestling with his passions; till I have bent myself into the posture of his hunched and peering hatred; till I see the world with his bloodshot and squinting eyes, looking between the blinkers of his half-witted concentration; looking up the short and sharp perspective of a straight road to a pool of blood, till I am really a murderer. ("The Secret of Father Brown")[102]

In "The Musgrave Ritual" and "The Retired Colourman," Holmes confessed to a similar imaginative methodology. But his clearest admission was in the 1939 film *Hound of the Baskervilles*, when Basil Rathbone's Holmes explains his diagnosis of:

Murder, my dear Watson. Refined, cold-blooded murder. There's no doubt about it in my mind, or perhaps I should say in my imagination, for that's where crimes are conceived and where they're solved—in the imagination.... That's why so many murders remain unsolved, Watson. People will stick to facts, even though they prove nothing. Now if we go beyond facts and use our imagination as the criminal does, imagine what might have happened, act upon it as I've been trying to do in this case, we usually find ourselves justified.[103]

The attempt to enshrine criminology as a science implies that crime is a distinct type of human activity and the criminal is a separate subspecies of human being. Bertillon's system of measurements and Lombroso's skull anomalies may seem laughable to moderns, but most psychiatric and psychological theories of the origins of criminality yield the same type of comforting class illusions. Thus, one of Chesterton's characters learns "from his books of criminology the one great discovery of that science, that mental and moral deformity are found only among poor people."[104] Doubtless much detective fiction is read and enjoyed for the implicit support it gives to a status quo in which the private detective represents that component of justice available only to those who can afford to pay for it. "Whoever reads a detective story about poor people? The poor have crimes; but the poor have no secrets. And it is because the proud have secrets that they need to be detected before they are forgiven" ("The Divine Detective").[105] Brown protests that there are no unimportant murder cases: "We matter to God—God only knows why. But that's the only possible justification of the existence of policemen.... The law really is right in a way, after all. If all men matter, all murders matter.... But, when once I step off that mystical level of equality, I don't see that most of your important murders are particularly important" ("The Quick One").[106]

Despite the tendency of Sherlockian scholars to identify many of Holmes's obscure clients as famous Victorian personages, the majority remain middle-class nonentities. Most notable cases involving heads of state were only indirectly alluded to by Watson. Holmes claimed "interest" to be a major factor in deciding whether to accept a case, and this led him to be involved, more often than any of his rivals, in noncriminal puzzles. With the wisdom of a serpent, Holmes recognized which "important" cases would advance his career while leaving him sufficient financial independence to remit his fees and serve the cause of justice.

Unlike Holmes, Chesterton's detective never complains of boredom; he is filled with wonder at criminal ingenuity: "A crime is like any other work of art. . . . the centre of it is simple, however much the fulfilment may be complicated" ("The Queer Feet").[107] The implication, according to Lynette Hunter, is that "the great criminals know that they lack interpretation and almost always seek the law or religion as an audience. They would jeopardise their own lives to have their crime examined as a work of art."[108] Not only is the humble detective an art critic, but he is the mystic who unravels the simple truth at the heart of the mystery, "the unrelenting sleuthhound who seeks to save and not slay" ("The Divine Detective").[109] In "The Adventure of the Veiled Lodger" Holmes becomes psychological counselor, father confessor, and pardoner: "Ruthless in the pursuit of criminals, he was very mild about their punishment" ("The Secret Garden").[110] The mystery of forgiveness is the only appropriate response to the mystery of evil. Such a divine detective, who "helped the criminal to escape by a plea of guilty," could never die. "Just as Arthur and Barbarossa were to return again, men felt that this preposterous detective must return again. He had emerged out of the unreality of literature into the glowing reality of legend, and in proof of this he has inherited the most widespread and pathetic of the characteristics of legendary heroes; that characteristic which makes men incredulous of their death" ("Sherlock Holmes").[111] And his tale would never be complete: "Even as a boy I believed there were some more pages that were torn out of my copy, and I am looking for them still. . . . And we should still have known that this was not really the story's end."[112]

The anemic fairies that Doyle came to believe in in his old age were pale shadows compared to that more solid childhood fairyland that Chesterton never ceased to inhabit. The hero-worshipping boy that survived and flourished in Chesterton (a comparison to Barrie's Peter Pan would be ponderously inappropriate) permitted a more accurate perception of the greatness and limitations of Sherlock Holmes than was allowed even to his creator. Father Brown is a critical commentary on Holmes: he is a love letter in fictional form from Chesterton to Conan Doyle's great sleuth. To Ronald Knox's Aquinas, Chesterton is the John of the Cross in the matter of Sherlock Holmes.

6
The Special Theory of Detection: The Semiology of Sherlock Holmes

All private detectives have eccentricities.
—Richard Wincor

From the claw guessing what size the beast must be
—Robert Burton

THE BIRTH AND DEATH OF THE HERO

Of his family I could obtain no satisfactory account.
—Poe, "A Tale of the Ragged Mountains"

Of my country and of my family I have little to say.
—Poe, "MS. Found in a Bottle"

Like many of Poe's characters, Holmes has no ancestry, no birth, no childhood, no education, no birthplace, no parentage, no family, no friends, no professional affiliations, no social connections—the exceptions to this litany can be counted on the fingers of one hand. This absence of all the usual expressions of rootedness serves to highlight the detective's cerebral activity and identify him more exclusively with his function.

This lack of origins will concern only those who mistake origins for explanations. The "genetic fallacy" explains away phenomena by reducing them to their beginnings.[113] In the exercise of this kind of simplistic reductionism, creative genius becomes nothing but a reflection of the unresolved conflict surrounding real or imagined childhood trauma. Alternatively, the great detective might be viewed as the logical culmination of hypothetical blue-blood genetic strains intersecting with certain upper class educational advantages. Stripped of all the trappings that allow such facile armchair analysis, Holmes forces the reader to concentrate on the problems immediately at hand. In sixty stories he has not left sufficient clues to even begin to reconstruct his educational background.

Early in their acquaintance, Watson considered Holmes to be relatively uneducated, but as their association continued, the great detective revealed himself to a published author, rare book collector, and accomplished violinist with wide expertise in many areas of learning: acting, anatomy, anthropology, archeology, ballistics, beekeeping, botany, bridge, cardiology, chemistry, chess, cosmology, criminology, cryptography, disguise, dermatoglyphics, dermatology, fencing, genetics, geology, graphology, history, languages, law, linguistics, literature, logic, microscopy, minerology, musicology, occupational medicine, ornithology, otolaryngology, philosophy, physics, psychology, pugilism, sensational literature, tobacco, tracking, and weapons. The vast range of this erudition has little or nothing to do with formal education. Indeed it speaks an eloquent argument for the opposite conclusion: Holmes is a superb example of the autodidact. The unevenness of his genius, its occasional blind spots, reveal the self-educated man. That his archenemy was a famous university professor further hints at some antipathy toward the prevailing system of formal education.

> He rose because men wanted him to be
> —Wallace Stevens

> For one must die to become a legend
> —Helen Waddell

> I still live
> —John Carter

Ronald Knox identified the alpenstock left behind at the Reichenbach Falls as an echo of Empedocles' sandal on Etna. This hypothesis is reinforced when it is recalled that Empedocles (who philosophized in verse) was the reputed inventor of deduction. But Holmes's death is peculiarly located in the middle of his professional career. This central position seems to materially emphasize some special mythic significance. If the death of the hero is needed to conclude his story and complete the cycle, then the hero who has no definite birth can have no real death; his story can never be complete, his tale is never ended.

On his return Holmes weakly explained this three-year absence by vague references to the exploits of a Norwegian explorer named Sigerson[114] and some researches into coal tar derivatives at

Montpellier; scholars have tracked his wanderings as far as Tibet, Persia, Mecca, Khartoum, and the Americas. But for his death to be interpreted as ritual repetition, one must look elsewhere for Holmes's activities. Since heroes like Hercules and Perseus are immortalized in starry constellations, a logical place to explore is the heavens.

The hiatus in Holmes's detective career lasted from 1891 to 1894. "The Final Problem" recording his death was penned by Doyle in 1893. In 1892 a new short period comet was first sighted. *Holmes's comet*[115] initially had a period of 6.9 years but in 1908 it increased to 7.3 years:

P 7.35 (period in Gaussian years)

e 0.379 (eccentricity of the orbit)

q 2.347 (perihelion distance in astronomical units)

ω 21.8 (argument of perihelion)

Ω 329.6 (longevity of ascending node)

i 19.5 (inclination)

It seems most appropriate that Holmes's constellation be episodic and eccentric, repetitive and of varying brilliance. And the only part of a comet that is visible is the tail; the rest must be deduced.

CHOOSING DAME OCUPACYON

> It is very seldom that an individual invents the occupation to which he will dedicate his life. That which—using a concept more dazzling than accurate—we call "genius" means (and really it means just this) the ability to invent one's own occupation.
> —Ortega y Gasset, *Interpretation of Universal History*

> He who would fight for the right . . . must have a private station and not a public one.
> —Socrates, *Apology*

Scholars recognize that Mycroft Holmes created his own unique job—whatever it was he actually did—and that he was the first (and quite probably the last) professional to fill that occupational niche. Through some kind of stupendous oversight it seems to have been inexplicably missed that Sherlock Holmes himself falls into the same category as his brother: he created his own profession. He was the world's first, and only, consulting private detective—"I suppose I am the only one in the world" *(A Study in Scarlet)*. Critics seeking to establish imaginary literary genealogies will find detectives in all ages. But Holmes was neither an amateur nor a policeman (as were the overwhelming majority of his predecessors and followers), and when his consulting status is taken into account the few remaining contenders for an identical occupation will be removed from the zone of consideration. (The "private" nature of Holmes's investigations is critical in another sense: science can only deal with data that can be made "public." Despite Holmes's frequent and exaggerated claims for the science of detection, the subject matter he has chosen to apply it to is eminently unscientific.)

Sherlock Holmes was not only the world's first private consulting detective; he was also (at least to the present time)—the last. Holmes knew he was the first and claimed to be founding a new profession. But his lessons in deductive reasoning were assuredly lost on both the official police and the dense Doctor Watson. His many descendants mimicked his eccentricities and mannerisms but failed to catch the spirit that illuminated his method. They didn't view detection as an

Table 4
Characteristics of the Professional Role in Consulting Occupations such as Medicine and Private Detection.

The traits listed are both idealistic and contradictory; individual professionals, and occasionally whole professions, will not infrequently delete certain characteristics (e.g., law and ethics).[116]

1. Apprenticeship: prolonged specialized training in a body of abstract knowledge
   an educationally communicable technique
2. Objectivity: essentially intellectual operation
   raw material derived from science and learning
   affectively neutral
3. Subjectivity: practical application, definite end
   action as opposed to knowledge orientation
   ideographic/pragmatic thinking
4. Autonomy: self-organization and self-regulation
   self-determination of training, standards, licensure, fees
   freedom from lay interference
5. Altruism: service orientation
   motivated by what is right not what is profitable
   intrinsic rewards: honor, prestige, public confidence
6. Ethics: trustworthy
   access to the most personal and intimate details
   empathy toward pain and suffering
7. Authority: the successful claim of emergency by expertise overrides, suspends, and destroys the rival claims of order, the normal, the routine, the rational and the legal.

almost sacred calling (table 4), a vocation to direct one's life's work and organize accidents.

A modern detective will have at his disposal more of the science that Holmes extolled, but the adventures of the former will attract less of a reading audience than those of his primitive forebear. As a teacher, as the pioneer of a new subspecialty, Sherlock Holmes was a complete and dismal failure. His encyclopedic textbook on crime remains unwritten, probably because as time went on he came to realize that the small fraction that "criminology" contributed to the science of detection had little to do with his true art and skill. A more predictable and manipulable species—*Apis melliferus*—became the subject of his last scientific monograph, a manual on beekeeping. His isolated criminal genius remained without legitimate progeny. In the same manner, the unique clinical skills of many practicing physicians die with them.

ARTIST, CRITIC, DANDY

> All primary observers are artists in their special science.
> —Doolin, *Wayfarers in Medicine*

> A painting is a thing which requires as much cunning, rascality and viciousness as the perpetration of a crime
> —Degas

Hippocrates had cautioned the physician against adopting a strange, luxurious, or elaborate professional dress. Although Doyle's written text described Holmes's costume as fairly conservative, Sidney Paget's original drawings introduced a somewhat greater degree of eccentricity. But with William Gillette's stage performances an exaggerated Bohemianism became the rule for later representations of Holmes in the media, and standard livery for detectives was henceforth obligatorily outlandish. His almost ridiculous attire accented certain Byronic strains in Holmes's character and served to link the antisocial scientific detective to the antisocial artist and aesthete—the dandy.

While the British conception of the "exquisite" or "swell" was almost exclusively sartorial and superficial, in continental romanticism the dandy's studied elegance was only a symbol for the aristocratic superiority of his mind. Baudelaire's *le dandy* took pleasure in astonishing and pride in never being astonished; his outward appearance mirrored an intense inward discipline.[117] This ideal was portrayed against a requisite background of decadence: dandyism was seen as the last flare of heroism in an age of decline. In his essay "On Murder Considered as One of the Fine Arts," Thomas De Quincey listed a number of great artists who "made it a rule never to practise their art but in full dress";[118] with the appropriate clothes to signal their professional roles, the painter, the art critic, even that critic of sublime criminal performances that is the detective, all flaunt the uniqueness of their specialization.

To balance off the striking costume that immediately identified him as the world's greatest detective, Holmes also perfected the art of disguise to the extent that the good Dr. Watson was never able to penetrate even a single one of Holmes's assumed identities. These carefully crafted alternative personae always seem to have something criminal about them: their purpose is concealment, trickery, deceit. Resort to disguise and role playing may also suggest a desire for anonymity, ironic detachment, a passion for privacy, a fear of commitment, even a horror of self. Whatever the psychiatric interpretation imposed, this recourse to multiple identities definitely places Holmes outside any acceptable Victorian frame of reference. He doesn't just use this art as another tool for thief-taking: he is an absolute master of it, with a relish that goes beyond the disreputably theatrical. Like the brief episodic narratives that make up his biography, the assumption of numerous disguises further fragments Holmes's identity, makes him more elusive to the chronicler of linear structures, and again reveals him as a repetitive mythic figure.

THE OBSERVATIONAL HOLMES

> Holmes was a meticulous, obsessional observer.
> —Critchley, *The Divine Banquet of the Brain*

> Any sufficiently advanced technology is indistinguishable from magic.
> —Clarke's Third Law

> That's what I call a self-evident proposition.
> —Sam Weller

A trait that Holmes derived from Laplace's *Mécanique Céleste* was the latter's frequent use of the phrase *"il est aisé à voir"* ("It is easy to see" or "Elementary, my dear reader") when he had omitted all the difficult intermediate steps and wanted to dazzle his audience with conclusions that were not at all obvious.[119] In "The Dancing Men" Holmes demonstrated his understsanding of this manipulation: "It is not really difficult to construct a series of inferences, each dependent upon its predecessor and each simple in itself. If, after doing so, one simply knocks out all the central inferences and presents one's audience with the starting-point and the conclusion, one may produce a startling, though possibly a meretricious, effect." The misleading impression Holmes feared was that this abbreviated sequence would be interpreted as a magic trick rather than a scientific process. Now magic and science are not that discrepant: both are experiential and both aim at transformations that give the illusion of understanding and controlling reality. The magician is the magister, the masterful and cunning man; mystery is a corruption of mastery. In the ancient world the forensic science *par excellence* was rhetoric, and one of the most powerful of rhetorical devices was the enthymeme, the syllogism in which crucial steps were omitted to enhance the dramatic effect of the argument.

One of the founders of modern neuropsychiatry, Jean-Martin Charcot (1825–93),[120] was noted for his artistic temperament. Apart from a gift for caricature, he was a *visuel* who would look again and again at a difficult case until it suddenly came together. With a single rapid glance, his diagnoses were unerringly accurate. But then medical syndromes are like perceptual models: they are statistical groupings or scientific hypotheses as to why signs and symptoms occur together.

Holmes stressed the visual component to his deductive skills through his use of a magnifying glass. Those commentators who wish to interpret this purely symbolic gesture as an indication of visual defect ("tobacco amblyopia") should be forewarned that dermatologists (a species not unknown to the ex-medical man Doyle), young and old, regardless of visual acuity, often employ a hand lens as an occupational signum. After all, stethoscopes, electrocardiograph machines, cathode ray tubes and all that other impressive medical paraphernalia are of little use to the poor dermatologist to affirm his technological expertise, and skin biopsies are too rare for that purpose. So, like Holmes, he accents the fact that his professional function is exercised in a highly specialized type of looking by using a child's magnifying glass.

ARROGANCE

Though a very great man, conscious of his qualities, Holmes was modest to a fault.

—Macdonald Critchley

The Special Theory of Detection

> This Dante because of his wisdom was somewhat arrogant, haughty, and disdainful, and as an overwhelming philosopher he did not know how to talk with common men.
> —Villani, *Cronica* 9

> Do all you can for the poor—but get all you can from the rich.
> —Lanfranc

In his George W. Gay lecture on arrogance, Franz Ingelfinger[121] distinguishes the beneficial arrogance of expertise from the destructive arrogance of ignorance. Beneficial arrogance is characterized as self-effacing, empathic, and courteous; the authoritarianism, paternalism, and domination required by the physician's professional role is only communicated with compassion and sympathy. In contrast, destructive arrogance is marked by vanity and presumption, arbitrary rudeness and a lack of empathy, its affective tone insolent and condescending. While recognizing that little is known with certainty (Dr. Ingelfinger's virtue of sophrosyne), the truly scientific physician also realizes that much of the success of medical practice is due to a certain style of doctor-patient interaction. Sherlock Holmes is often criticized for his brisk, cold, undisturbed, and even slightly brutal—and, yes, arrogant—professional manner; it differs little from the impassive professionalism of the busy surgeon. Cancer or crime must be eradicated as quickly and efficiently as possible. The patient's/client's feelings, however, must neither be ignored nor allowed to interfere; they will have significant impact on compliance and outcome, and their cooperation must, therefore, be enlisted.

In the opening framing sequence to most of the tales, Holmes makes a series of brilliant deductions about his client's past history and recent travels (i.e., the mode of transportation and the route followed to 221 B Baker Street)—irrelevant and insignificant details, like the pediatrician who informs the mother of a carotinemic infant that the baby prefers yellow vegetables—all before the client or mother can utter a word. "I have found it wise to impress my clients with a sense of power." Almost without exception, no single case hinges on this opening display of cerebral fireworks, and it is rarely repeated later in the story. But having secured his client's unshaken belief that the sleuth's omniscience extends to areas of greater significance, he then proceeds to listen to a long, detailed account of the problem, flawlessly narrated by an emotionally troubled—though temporarily calmed by the great detective's reassuring attention—prospective client. The trusting attitude implanted with his opening diagnostic remarks is cemented by the care with which he attends the patient's tangled tale. By hearing the client out—an interrupting question is rare—he earns the right to take control of the situation and apply guidelines derived from his experience. The advice that follows is concrete and practical but very open ended and contributes little to the problem's ultimate solution: it capitalizes on the client's trust and requires them to await the outcome of certain tests, investigations, and other events. The professional taking the time to listen becomes a symbolic lesson in patience. Holmes's client-centered ventilation therapy is a more enduring model for the practitioner than his deductions from dust and ashes. Doctors need to listen to their patients more.

When his arrogance assumes a more destructive tone, it is directed more to Holmes's coprofessionals—the bumbling official police—and occasionally to his wealthier and more powerful clients who wish to control or limit the direction and extent of his investigations. His interactions with the poor are marked by a deeper sensitivity. "My professional charges are upon a fixed scale. I do not vary them, save when I remit them altogether." Holmes is able with grace and courtesy to follow the Hippocratic maxim, "Sometimes give your services for nothing. For where there is love of man, there is also love of the art."

THE FINAL PROBLEM: AN EVIL GENIUS

> An end of evil in a profounder logic
> —Wallace Stevens

> since where the one is,
> its arch enemy cannot be missing
> —Marianne Moore

> You think that you understand divine things, and holiness and unholiness, so accurately that, in such a case as you have stated, you can bring your father to justice without fear that you yourself may be doing an unholy deed?
> —Socrates, *Euthyphro*

> And Brain, and Brain alone, shall rule the world!
> —C. L. Dodgson

A reductionist approach to genius and creativity is not the exclusive property of either Bacon or Freud. The von Däniken school of antihistorical analysis would explain away any signs of precocious genius in the ancient world as alien intervention from beyond the stars. Discrepant cultural phenomena that are not easily accounted for by the standard textbook mechanism of gradual evolution are rationalized as evidence for extraterrestrial visitations. The genius of Sherlock Holmes, Leonardo da Vinci, and others can also be reduced to the common level by viewing them as time travelers from outer space or the future—very ordinary men who simply happen to be equipped with a more advanced technology that was slowly developed by a long series of other very ordinary technicians. Another way for the small-minded critic to cut genius down to size is to equate intellectual superiority with evil and madness. Holmes will be proved to be identical with Moriarity or Jack the Ripper on the basis of their cunning proficiency in matters criminal. A certain degree of difficulty in distinguishing the detective from the criminal would seem to be inherent in the qualities associated with the two roles.

Oedipus, Hamlet, and the three princes of Serendip are all riddle-solving royal offspring forced to investigate the actual or attempted murder of the father/king/emperor. As the suggestion of incest weakens, so does the identification of the detective with the murderer: Oedipus fulfills the Delphic oracle's prophecy by his unwitting patricide/regicide; Hamlet's uncle is guilty of the premeditated fratricide/regicide of Hamlet senior, but with Michele Tramezzino's Renaissance retelling of the myth, the detective/son has been fragmented into three princes, the royal father has been transposed to the emperor of a neighboring kingdom, and the putative murderer is an unrelated courtier (distraught about his own son's fate at the hands of the monarchy). The identification of the detective with the murderer has thinned out even more (along with the relationship of royalty) by the time Voltaire, Dumas, and Poe reworked their versions of the trickster theme. Many of the earliest detectives, such as the Bow Street Runners and the Bobbies, were little better than criminals, and the bureaucratic inefficiency of the modern official police often makes them unwitting accomplices. Evil tends to banality, and organized evil—as witnessed in John Gardner's linguistically interesting and superficially inventive Moriarity novels—is uninspired and, compared to the original Holmes tales, uninteresting.

Plato's Phaedrus held the prophet (*mantike*) or genius to be akin to the madman (*manike*), and Seneca's "*nullum magnum ingenium sine mixtura dementiae*" was translated by Dryden as "great wits are sure to madness near allied." The association of genius with madness or evil is a recurrent motif in literature: Dupin referred to his arch-enemy, Minister D-, as "that *monstrum horrendum,* an unprincipled man of genius." Moriarity's genius was reflected both in his invisible criminal network as well as his authorship of *The Dynamics of an Asteroid*.[122] No copies of this famous work survive, but scholars estimate its publication date at around 1875. Of interest is the fact that in 1865 another mathematics professor, Charles Lutwidge Dodgson, penned *The Dynamics of a Parti-cle*, a work later collected in *Notes by an Oxford Chiel*, published in 1874. This Oxford clergyman evidenced a lifelong interest in the paradoxes of logic and the practical limits of reason. (Several other Holmes-Carroll links are noted in the last section of this chapter.)

Holmes's perfectly legal use of cocaine to relieve his periods of boredom is taken as supporting possible criminal tendencies. Account would have to be taken of the brilliant achievement of the American surgeon Dr. William Stewart Halsted (1852–1922), one of the founders of the Johns Hopkins Medical School. Dr. Halsted became addicted to cocaine in the 1870s, broke this habit with morphine, and then completed a long, active and productive medical career as a lifelong morphine addict.[123]

Doyle compared both Holmes and Moriarity to spiders manipulating filaments at the centers of their webs. This predatory image of control was used by Jean Cocteau in his play *The Knights of the Round Table* to accent the evil brilliance of an intelligence akin to sorcery: "I was often warned in those days against a certain old magician. When he takes a place over, he puts it to sleep and lays it waste by sucking the juices from all the living creatures in it. He lives there like a spider at the center of its web. His name is a rather curious one . . . Merlin."[124] Inhuman intelligence—"a brain without a heart, as deficient in human sympathy as he was preeminent in intelligence" ("The Greek Interpreter")—is perceived as the most dangerous thing in the world. Great knowledge is misinterpreted as the product of black magic—"You would certainly have been burned, had you lived a few centuries ago" ("A Scandal in Bohemia"). Thus the Middle Ages classified the Latin poet Virgil (Publius Vergilius Maro, 70–19 B.C.) and Pope Sylvester II (Gerbert of Aurillac, ca. 945–1003) as wizards.[125] By a coincidence of opposites, *corruptio optimi pessima*—Jung and Heraclitus's rule of "enantiodromia."

It is unfortunate that this misconception—the equation of intelligence with cold logical analysis and abstract reasoning—is often supported by the less creative members of the scientific establishment. The suggested identification of supreme intelligence with supreme evil rests on a fundamental misconception of the nature of intelligence. Are highly intelligent persons obliged to pursue their own ends divorced from humane considerations? Do selfish genes or professional education force the genius to act in ways repellent to common humanity?

The recent discoveries of fraud in scientific research have brought these issues to fresh prominence, but the public scandal raised by these episodes reveals the extent to which the history of scientific achievement has been rewritten in the popular mind to reflect a clear and logical (albeit imaginary) progression of discoveries made only by men (some more creative imagination) of the highest ethical standards. Downplaying the human frailties and frauds in science has the inevitable result of making even the most outstanding achievements seen inhuman.

The researcher or clinician who swallows this myth whole is afflicted with some degree of megalomania and then subjected to intense pressures to live up to an impossible dream. The lay person who has this chimera imposed on him is first pressured into servile obeisance and then responds with rage to an unfilled promise. Malpractice suits in medicine rarely involve a failure to use the latest technology; they are more frequently brought on by too great a readiness to employ such new toys, combined with an abysmal ignorance of basic human etiquette and courtesy.

THROUGH THE LOOKING-GLASS: ALICE'S UNDERWORLD ADVENTURES

> "Suppose he never commits the crime?" said Alice.
> —*Through the Looking-Glass*

> "A really brilliant addition to the great literature of nonsense."
> —Chesterton, "Sherlock Holmes"

The detective stories of Arthur Conan Doyle and the children's nonsense of Charles Lutwidge Dodgson were typically eccentric English tales narrated at one remove from their authors through the vehicles of Dr. John H. Watson and Lewis Carroll (1832–98). Their overwhelming popularity and assumed complexity gave rise to annotation industries that comprise independent segments of the publishing field. Holmes's fog-bound, gas-lit (distorted) London with its criminal underworld exhibits a striking resemblance to Alice's underground and looking-glass worlds. Like alternative (non-Euclidian) geometries, both universes maintain a certain internal consistency while propounding an archaic or at least unusual logic of, in part, chivalry and knight-errantry.

These authors displayed a photographic attention to detail and a detailed attention to photography. Their universes have a nightmarish quality about them, with crime and nonsense representing different types of bizarre and seemingly inexplicable behavior. The major problems presented center on questions of identity and the distinction of reality from appearance. The hero/heroine starts from and returns to a home setting of hobbitlike comfort and undertakes an unconnected series of poetry-filled adventures to deduce the solutions to criminal puzzles or logical conundra. Language itself plays such a prominent role that, like time in Proust, it takes on the aspect of an independent character. The element of play—adventure released from the seriousness of time—pervades the chess/Wittgensteinian problem of discovering the rules of a game by observation.

For Lewis Carroll there was something unjust in the fact that little girls grew up; for Conan Doyle the loss of childhood innocence could perhaps be redressed (if not recaptured) by detecting the guilty criminal. The characters that people their narratives are archetypal but sexually uninvolved or immature and, therefore, defenseless before facile Freudian psychobabble. (In an age that panders to child pornography as an art form, we may yet look forward to a Holmes pastiche in which a mathematics don at Christ Church, Oxford, who has a predilection for photographing little girls in the nude, is cleared of charges of child abuse and sexual molestation and a scandal is hushed up, one in which the rakish Prince of Wales and/or one of his cronies has been playing out a Gilles de Raiz with innocent children—all recounted with nauseating detail.)

Wellman suggested that Mrs. Hudson was actually an attractive young widow;[126] Rex Stout postulated that Watson was a woman. With no surviving records of Holmes's youth, consideration must be given to the fact that if Alice were ever to escape Carroll's timeless universe and mature, there is little doubt that she would grow up to be—Sherlock Holmes.

7
The Book of Watson: An Uncertain Friendship

animae dimidium meae
—Horace

I tell you the labor is too much for one. Two must share it.
Shaw, *Back to Methuselah*

"One can't, perhaps," said Humpty Dumpty; "but two can."
—*Through the Looking-Glass*

And if Dr. Watson wasn't with you it wouldn't seem as if you were detecting at all.
—Gillette, *The Painful Predicament of Sherlock Holmes*

A PICKWICKIAN SYNDROME

A good many stagnant, stupid-seeming people are a great deal deeper than the length of your intellectual walking-stick.
—Holmes, *Poet at the Breakfast Table*

In Arthur Whitaker's Holmesian pastiche, "The Case of the Man Who Was Wanted," the following exchange of dialogue takes place:

Holmes: "the most interesting cases do not always present the most bizarre features at the outset."
Watson: "'So far from it, on the contrary, quite the reverse,' to quote Sam Weller."[127]

This is one of the few printed texts to suggest a relationship between John Watson and Sam Weller. Dickens certainly described a very Holmesian Mr. Pickwick: "an observer of human nature" (chapter 2)[128] who displays "that perfect coolness and self-possession, which are the indispensible accompaniments of a great mind" (chaper 4); he is "a quick and powerful reasoner" (chapter 10) with a "well regulated mind" (chapter 16). Like Holmes, he uses his observational skills to note "the appearance, and speculate upon the character and pursuits of the persons by whom he was surrounded—a habit in which he in common with many other great men delighted to indulge" (chapter 6). Holmes does not accept supernatural explanations—"there is nothing of the marvellous in what I am going to relate" (chapter 3), and the adventures of Holmes and Watson have as their substrate human tragedy: "we seem destined to enter no man's house without involving him in some degree of trouble" (chapter 18). Pickwick collects scientific observations: "The labours of others have raised for us an immense reservoir of important facts" (chapter 4), but he is acutely aware of the difficulties inherent in applied science: "many of the best and ablest philosophers, who have been perfect lights of science in matters of theory, have been wholly unable to reduce them to practice" (chapter 19).

Pickwick's scientific prowess is, of course, pompously overestimated to the point of ridiculousness; the only thing that gives him any semblance of credibility is his status as a gentleman. Holmes would later make even more outrageous claims to scientific omniscience and (almost) carry them off. Pickwick's greatest discovery remains Sam Weller: "between ourselves, I flatter myself he is an original, and I am rather proud of him" (chapter 22). But what is it about Weller, that "regular thorough-bred original" (chapter 42), that indissolubly links his fate to that of Pickwick?

> "What ud become on you vithout me?
> It can't be done, sir, it can't be done."
> (chapter 56)

THE ANALYSAND OF FATE

> The wish to be friends is a quick growth, but friendship is not.
> —Aristotle

> They became old friends at once.
> —Romain Rolland, *Jean Christophe*

> For all acts but generation, man would have been better off with another man as his helpmate.
> —Aquinas

> Above all, I am faithful.
> —Sancho Panza

Lipot Szondi proposed a theory of personality or "fate analysis" in which an individual's character traits stem from the familial unconscious.[129] His hypothesis represented an unsuccessful marriage of Jungian depth psychology with quantitative genetic analysis. When empirical validation proved overwhelmingly negative, his "experimental diagnostics of drives" fell into well-deserved neglect, but as an application of mythology to the life of the individual it suggested a genetic basis to apparently chance friendships. Collectively unconscious (genetically recessive) drives in reality determine what superficially appear to be an attraction between opposites.

When Stamford first introduced Watson and Holmes to effect a room-sharing arrangement, there was an immediate chemical reaction between the two, the one "a good, honest unthinking Shandean" person and capable of understanding the obvious only when it was carefully explained to him, and the other self-trained in the perception of subtleties; the one something of a womanizer and lazy, the other something of a misanthrope and a workaholic. Holmes cultivates the acquaintance of a lower species, boobus Britannicus (played to perfection by Nigel Bruce), so well described by Roger Beadon: "And how typically were his qualities those which Englishmen like to claim as their own—reticence, aversion to publicity, abhorrence of the theatrical, and the sense that, in the great moments of life, it should be thought only to do faithfully, leaving glory to follow good deeds." When the two of them are inactive (and often even when they are working on a case together) their relationship appears comical because of superficial communication difficulties. Their friendship, however, is situated in silence and solitude—"You have a grand gift of silence, Watson. It makes you quite invaluable as a companion" ("The Man with the Twisted Lip"). Holmes and Watson, both eccentrics, allow each other space to be themselves. The elective affinity between the doctor and the detective is rooted pure and simply in a common love of justice. The part played by financial and emotional considerations is overshadowed by the more basic concerns noted by Aristotle over two millennia ago: "the highest form of justice seems to have an element of friendly feeling in it. . . . The perfect form of friendship is that between the good, and those who resemble each other in virtue. . . . Friendship and justice exist between the same persons and are co-extensive in range."[130] In the service of individual patients and clients, the love of justice becomes a passion for equity; and in this light it is significant to recall that Holmes is dramatically absurd as a theoretician and Watson verges on incompetence as a practitioner, saved only by a good bedside manner.

A CLERKES TALES

Selon le clerc est deu le maistre
—Villon

I once did hold it, as our statists do,
A baseness to write fair, and labour'd much
How to forget that learning.
—*Hamlet V*

Mr. Pickwick, with that anxious desire to abstain from giving offence to any, and with those delicate feelings for which all who knew him well know he was so eminently remarkable, purposely substituted a fictitious designation, for the real name of the place in which his observations were made . . . concealing even the direction in which the burough is situated.
—Dickens, *Pickwick Papers*

The popularity of the Sherlock Holmes stories has survived the decline of British imperialism and English letters. Readers ignorant of the Victorian Age in literature and totally uninterested in the more obscure antecedents of the detective novel will nevertheless be found to be intimately conversant with such places as the Grimpen Mire, Abbey Grange, the Diogenes Club, Godolphin Street, Marcini's Restaurant, Laburnum Vale, Pondicherry Lodge, Stoke Moran, Ridling Thorpe Manor, Shosombe Old Place, and Wisteria Lodge. With a reasonable percentage of identifiable locators, Dr. John H. Watson has deliberately mixed in a steady stream of familiar-sounding proper nouns that are not to be found on any map or in any peerage of England, ancient or modern. Theories abound to explain this mythopoetic litany: (1) his Hippocratic oath supported the professional secret (the sacred inviolability of the doctor-patient/detective-client confidentiality), and forbade gossiping regardless of the source of the information; (2) his fear of political or personal repercussions upon revealing classified information; (3) his total fabrication of some of the tales—Holmes considered most of the stories sufficiently distant from scientific truth to be classified as fictitious. These hypotheses presume that Watson's verbal transformations are deliberate; a fourth (though highly unlikely) possibility is that the good doctor suffered from a subclavian steal syndrome in which a vascular obstruction siphons blood from the vertebral-basilar arterial system thus causing cerebral ischemia with the attendant symptoms of forgetfulness, mental confusion, fatigue, and fainting. Attractive as this last theory is in that it would help us understand why Watson did not seem able to remember even the exact location of his war wounds received in the Afghan campaign, it fails to explain a much more striking quality of Watson's extensive use of neologisms that cannot result from a mere transient amnesia, aphasia, or lalopathy: in the science of onomastics, the fine art of coining names, Watson/Doyle has for his peers Lucan, Dante, Milton, and Tolkien. Such use of proper names are what Auden called poetry in the raw. This aesthetic effect is so overwhelming that these fabricated names have actually been very effectively employed in T. S. Eliot's "East Coker":

> . . . not only in the middle of the way
> But all the way, in a dark wood, in a bramble,
> On the edge of a grimpen, where is no secure foothold,
> And menaced by monsters, fancy lights,
> Risking enchantment.[131]

Samuel Rosenberg provides some fascinating Freudian interpretations for Doyle's nominal transforms, but these contribute little toward understanding the universal resonance, the romantic lure and attraction of faraway places with strange sounding names.[132] As Proust noted repeatedly in *Remembrance of Things Past*, all sorts of associations are drawn to imaginary names of persons and places that are almost real—and sometimes more than real.

Despite numerous attempts at Sherlockian chronologies, Watson is no better at dates than at place names. With David Copperfield, the good doctor can say, "I don't profess to be clear about dates." This repeated and deliberate blurring of time zones suggests, like so many other structures in the Holmes canon, that one is dealing with mythic (or timeless) time.

FALSTAFF

> Who was Watson? I do not mean the bumbling ass that is Hollywood's conception. I mean the *real* Watson of whom my father said to me in so many words on more than one occasion—"those who consider Watson to be a fool are

simply admitting that they haven't read the stories attentively". . . . Certainly Watson was no fool.
—Adrian Conan Doyle

"There is no one who knows the higher criminal world of London so well as I do."
—"The Final Problem"

Harry Monmouth, you see, was essentially an actor. Without a role, he was nothing.
—Robert Nye, *Falstaff*

There are many critics who think that Dr. John Watson's reputation has suffered a fate similar to that of Sir John Fastolf, a well to do professional soldier in the first half of the fifteenth century. Sir John was one of the most famous English captains in the Hundred Years War, but his fame was curiously distorted by his last-minute appearance in the history plays of Shakespeare.[133] In the earliest version of *Henry IV*, the fat knight who was a "villainous abominable misleader of youth" (the latter in the person of the riotous Prince Hal) was named Sir John Oldcastle. But the historic Sir John had a direct descendant, Lord Cobham, who happened to be the lord chamberlain, and his complaints required Shakespeare to rechristen his obese protagonist Falstaff. Although Sir John Fastolf was also a historic personage, he had no descendants to protest. The factual record of Sir John's life offers little support for Shakespeare's almost slanderous portrait of "the fat knight with the great belly-doublet: he was full of jests, and gripes, and knaveries and mocks." Holinshed followed the chronicler Monstrelet's hostile interpretation of Fastolf's conduct at the battle of Pataie (Patay)—"From this battell departed without anie stroke striken sir Iohn Fastolfe"—which charge, however unfounded, gave rise to one of the great comic scenes in Shakespeare.

Apart from the transformation of a dignified and conservative professional military officer who had served his country under fire into a buffoon of gigantic proportions—"a liar, a braggart, a 'bag of guts,' a wit, a friend of rogues and ne-er-do-wells"—Falstaff offers the possibility of another comparison with John H. Watson, M.D., late of her imperial majesty's Fifth Northumberland Fusiliers and Princess Charlotte of Wales's Royal Berkshire Regiment. For both clowns are denied any independent existence—in *The Merry Wives of Windsor*, Sir John stumbles and falters with only traces of his exuberant language remaining. He lives only when he interacts with Hal/Holmes, Prince Hal who acts out first his worldly vices and then his royal pantomime with the disinterest of a consummate actor:

> The prince but studies his companions
> Like a strange tongue, wherein, to gain the language,
> 'Tis needful that the most immodest word
> Be look'd upon, and learn'd; which once attain'd,
> Your Highness knows, comes to no further use
> But to be known and hated. So, like gross terms,
> The prince will in the perfectness of time
> Cast off his followers; and their memory
> Shall as a pattern or a measure live,
> By which his Grace must mete the lives of others,
> Turning past evils to advantages.
>
> (*2 Henry IV*, 4.4.68–78)

Many commentators have noted Holmes's often cold aloofness to Watson—"I am the most offending soul alive"—and especially their unexplained separations during both the great hiatus and Holmes's retirement to beekeeping in Sussex. The evolutionary pattern of their friendship matches quite closely the development of the relationship between Hal and Falstaff. But the complementarity of the Machiavellian and dispassionate calculation of Hal/Holmes with the bumbling earthiness of Sir John/Doctor John will remain unclear unless the significance of these unofficial court jesters is uncovered.

When Prince Hal becomes Henry V—"the mirror of all Christian kings"—he puts aside his friendship with Falstaff. What has he gained from this association? If Shakespeare's political purpose was to legitimize Henry, the relationship with Falstaff cannot be viewed as mere comic relief. Auden interpreted Henry V's wordliness as representative of the temporal order of Justice and Falstaff's unworldliness as a comic symbol of the supernatural order of charity. Falstaff is the eternal spirit of childhood with its urgent physical appetites, its inability to delay gratification, and its ignorance of time—"What a devil hast thou to do with the time of day?" If Henry is Justice, then Falstaff must be Justice *plus* Mercy; Falstaff/Watson is the larger, more encompassing figure, only appearing simpler because uncluttered by the complex developments associated with being born, having a history, and dying. (The unreality of Falstaff's death is highlighted when it occurs off-stage.)

THE FOOL

> There is no character in comedy which requires so much ingenuity as that of the fool; for he must not in reality be what he appears.
>
> —*Don Quixote*

Folk tales have always tended to view the hakham, the clever man, with suspicion and sympathize more with the tam, the fool. Arrogance and ambition make the intelligent person skeptical and ultimately miserable; he becomes so critical that nothing can please or satisfy. The tam, in contrast, remains simple enough to attain wisdom and joy from life. Watson does not fit the classic distinction between the schlemiel and the schlimazl, but then he is his own special kind of fool, inseparable from his shadowy twin. (If Watson is to Sherlock as Sherlock is to Mycroft, where does Moriarity fit in?)

In Wu Ch'êng-ên's sixteenth-century popular novel *Hsi Yu Ki*, the central figure, Monkey, stands for the restless instability of genius.[134] To restrain his Holmesian intellectual arrogance, Monkey is obliged to use his almost magical powers to right the wrongs of the oppressed in a series of fantastic adventures. His extreme personality traits are carefully balanced by a triumvirate of Watsonian companions: Tripitaka, a simple man who blunders anxiously through the vicissitudes of life; Pigsy, who represents the physical appetites and a "kind of cumbrous patience"; and Sandy, an ill-defined and colorless character who symbolizes ch'êng, "sincerity." In this psychomachy, it takes only one figure to represent Holmes but three to cover the pantheon of typically Watsonian traits. The common man may well be more complex than the clever man, much more difficult to track down in his many guises. Tripitaka, Sandy, Sancho Panza, Sam Weller, Falstaff—the wisdom of the fool is deeper than the knowledge of the wise.

A FEMALE WATSON

> The parody best proves the real thing.
> —Brendan Kennelly, "The Hunchback"

Few modern versions of the Sherlock Holmes myth have come closer to catching the spirit of the original than James Goldman's play *They Might Be Giants*. An unbalanced retired judge, Justin Playfair (Justin, upright, the just one) believes he is Sherlock Holmes and comes under the care of a lady psychiatrist, Dr. Mildred Watson—"I can't remember how I lived before you came."[135] In the first demonstration of his powers, Justin performs the typical Holmesian mind reading act—on a mute psychotic inpatient in an asylum. This is a kind of limit case of identity in which the schizophrenic Mr. Small is revealed to be Rudolph Valentino. With a few thrusts of his rapier wit, Justin can strike through the mask much more effectively than the modern psychotherapeutic bureaucracy of power for the simple reason that he sincerely cares for the downtrodden Everyman (Mr. *Small*) who has escaped into the security of a dream world.

Justin's methodologic rules are vintage Holmes: "I work by pure deduction." "I don't believe in accidents. . . . There are two laws in life: all things are logical—they must make sense—and no things are exactly what they seem. Each accident is part of a design and every object has a secret side."[136] He is a consulting detective—"I've daily office hours. If you need a consultation, please feel free to call for an appointment"—and is familiar with the inverse of Poe's limited insight—"Which one? The most unlikely one; that's only logical."[137]

This is a passionately cerebral Holmes—"My life depends on what I think"[138]—whose intuitive approach to facts borders at times on a psychotic disconnection from reality—"Half the trick in finding clues is knowing that they're there."[139] Dr. Watson predictably diagnoses a classic case of paranoia in which "the victim's faculties grow keener, ultrasensitive. His intuition verges on the supernatural. He's capable of things that seem like genius."[140] But Justin has little concern for a reductionist psychiatry that has long ago given up trying to help people and instead has been transformed into one of the major forces of social repression: "You think I'm mad. You analysts are all alike. . . . Why is it analysts can't ever analyze."[141]

This Holmes is a visionary whose philosophy seems to have a great deal in common with the genre of the American Western: "If you look closely down there, Watson, you'll see principles. You'll see the possibility of justice and proportion. You can see men move their lives. There are no masses in Virginia City; only individuals whose will for good or bad can bring them to the ends they ought to have."[142] Justin's "view of things, complex in many ways, is very simple when it comes to values. Everything is vivid and extreme: it's very good or very bad, joyful or agonized, bright colored or sheer murk. And no two ways about it."[143]

The simple must not be confused with the simplistic. Ludwig Wittgenstein shared Justin's fondness for Western films and recognized that the ultimate source of values was not readily available to either philosophical analysis or psychoanalysis.[144] Justin stands for fair play: his deductive skill is completely subservient to his sense of justice. Holmesian intelligence is meant to change reality, to make it more just, even if that change appears paranoid and delusionary. And the female Dr. Watson represents the caring physician who sees through the diagnosis and the delusion to the truth in the patient and the delusion.

8
Conclusion: The Unified Field Theory of Detection

What is here is the end of adventures and the beginning of an Adventure.
—C. Daly King

Truth is not identical with repeatability; on the contrary, it is what absolutely cannot be duplicated.
—Friedrich Georg Juenger

Intellect does not attain its full force unless it attacks power.
—Madame de Stäel

A CASE OF IDENTITY: THE GOOD DETECTED

The Master would hardly be so well loved among all the great literary figures were he not so *good*.
—David Pearson

Not cold and hunger but Law and Justice are bitterest affliction of the poor.
—Sylvia Townsend Warner

The very word "justice" irritates scientists.
—Karl Menninger

Most people say it is the intellect which makes a great scientist. They are wrong: it is the character.
—Albert Einstein

Conclusion: The Unified Field Theory of Detection 107

Sherlock Holmes is eccentric in more than his personal idiosyncrasies. His very manner of thinking is eccentric—off the beaten path. In the rather fantastic business of the Red-headed League, Holmes twice moves off center, as it were, for a change in perspective that permits a solution to an otherwise unsolvable problem. Jabez Wilson asks why the expensive prank of the Red-headed League has been played on him. To this question no direct answer is possible. Holmes's approach is not that of a problem solver but rather of a problem finder: by asking a related but distinctly different question— why did the League of Red-headed Men want the pawnbroker away from his establishment for a set period of time—the resolution of the mystery becomes elementary, obvious even to a Watson.

But there is a second, infrequently noted ec-centricity about the case of the Red-headed League that revolves around the identity of the client Jabez Wilson—Jabez, "he will bring sorrow." The question of Mr. Wilson's identity cannot really be finally answered because, like most of Holmes's clients, he leaves few clues and passes quickly from the scene. It was, of course, a private Doyle joke to make the pawnbroker a Freemason and have him duped by a red-headed (namely, hatted) league (i.e., conspiracy) located at Pope's Court (alternatively identified as Mitre Court). The details that are revealed about this client are generally of an unsavory sort: Mr. Wilson is "not over-bright," he is greedy for his lost four pounds weekly, he is quite satisfied to employ an assistant at half wages, he is "an average commonplace British tradesman, obese, pompous, and slow," and he presumes himself eligible for some of Holmes's free "advice to poor folk who were in need of it." A distasteful money-grubbing nonentity if ever there were. Although the detective distinguishes the interest of the case from the interestingness of the client, Holmes's second decentration allows him to perceive a much more fundamental issue. If the bank robbery had been successful and the thieves had made a clean getaway, what would have been the fate of Mr. Jabez Wilson— the pawnbroker (scil., dealer in stolen goods) with a tunnel leading from the despoiled bank vault to his shop, an absconded apprentice, a recent unexplained financial windfall, and a ridiculous story about a league of red-headed men who get to copy out the *Encyclopaedia Britannica* for extravagant wages? In the absence of any other culprit there is little doubt that the gullible shopkeeper would have spent the short remainder of his life behind bars. Holmes's passion for justice must ultimately be identified with his concern for the individual; his eccentric perception enables him to strike through the mask of a Jabez Wilson to the reality of a John Watson. The real conclusion to the "Red-headed League" is finding the despicable Mr. Wilson not guilty/cured.

Holmes's clients are for the most part such victims. Doyle's imitators could never perceive the wisdom of De Quincey's observation that in the most artistic murders, the victim must needs be anonymous—a nonpublic figure; they are always involving the detective with the foibles of the famous. The physician who can always discover beneath the trivial complaint of the average patient a human being in need will be faithful to Osler's portrait of the ideal healer who treats patients rather than diseases. In practice Holmes adhered to this priority, always placing the client ahead of the crime. Since Doyle thought this lesson too simple, he continually made his detective exaggerate the esoteric aspects of the crime/disease. Yet readers continue to be more fascinated by the opening framing sequences in which the detective reveals to his prospective clients various details about their history and movements. In these confessional encounters, the mystery that is revealed is the innocence of the client.

SHERLOCK HOLMES AND MEDICINE

> Rule IV states clearly that the history must never be given; the physician must be made to extract it.
> —I. Rose, "The Professional Patient"

> Only a good man can be a great physician.
> —Hermann Nothnagel

Modern forensic science is capable of almost miraculously linking the criminal to his crime. Do citizens rest more comfortable and secure in the knowledge that the official police have such professional expertise at their disposal? Modern medicine is capable of technological marvels undreamed of a quarter century ago and has been accelerating this knowledge explosion at an exponential rate for almost a century. Do patients feel more comfortable and secure when they place themselves in the hands of modern scientific physicians who make their predecessors of less than two generations ago the technical equivalent of witch doctors? If medicine is a science and this science has made such outstanding strides, why hasn't medicine advanced in popular esteem?

The lesson that Sherlock Holmes has for modern medicine addresses these issues but tends to be obscured by a deceptive rhetoric, much of it coming directly from Holmes himself. His maxim about ruling out the impossible can certainly be interpreted as supporting the abominable practice of substituting a shotgun laboratory approach to diagnosis for common sense, patient-oriented clinical judgement. But that would be a misinterpretation. Although the detective is always talking of test tubes and chemicals, none of Holmes's cases hinges on a laboratory result. These mystery narratives depend instead on a detailed history and meticulous observation of the scene of the crime. In the early years of medical school the student hears repeated over and over again the maxim that three-fourths of all diagnoses come from the history, with the physical examination and laboratory data merely confirming the initial impression. Another 20 percent of diagnoses are made by physical findings with the laboratory supporting the clinician's reasoning. It seems a puzzling irony that as the student enters the clinical years, internship and residency, the reliance on laboratory, radiographic, and other special procedures increases. The young physician in training is more likely to be criticized for not ordering further tests than for not investing more time in reviewing the history and physical examination.

This situation should not really be surprising, for the physician in practice is financially rewarded almost exclusively on the basis of the use of specialized and expensive diagnostic and therapeutic procedures. Insurance companies are reluctant to reimburse anyone but the psychiatrist for talking with the patient. Yet the Holmesian ideal involves just that—to solve the case without ever leaving his sitting room—à la Nero Wolfe. Holmes, of course, does not hesitate to make house calls. The modern physician prefers for the patient to come to the clinic office where high technology is more readily available. But does the doctor/detective allow the time required to learn all about the physical and social milieu in which the disease occurs and in which it must be treated? How many physicians can describe the patient's family and work environments with the same facility that they read the computerized serum chemistry printout? That the diagnosis of emotional disorders or stress-related disease is made to depend on the prior exclusion of every conceivable organic diagnosis reflects irrational behavior and fosters the growth of numerous (and mostly absurd) alternative therapies under the rubric "holistic medicine."

The confusion of the roles of laboratory technician with that of healer stems from misclassifying medicine as a science. Not only is medicine not a theoretical science, but it is not even a practical science. Medicine uses science; it is scientific in its research methodology, in its critical approach to its eclectic subject matter. But medicine is not applied anatomy, applied biochemistry, applied physiology, or applied whatever. Medicine is part art, part craft, and part social activity; it is the art of caring for the sick as practiced by someone who has undergone an apprenticeship in relevant areas of ethics, clinical diagnostic skills, therapeusis, and behavioral and basic sciences.

HIS LAST BOW

> The tale still telling, never told.
> —George MacDonald

> The real actors on the stage of the universe are very few, if their adventures are many.
> —*Hamlet's Mill*

Despite their relatively recent arrival on the scene, Holmes and Watson's presence among the great figures of world literature has already inspired more imitations than any other literary characterizations. The pastiches and parodies, criticism and pseudo-scholarship that attend the Sherlock Holmes saga often resemble the discussion of a story around the campfire. The millions of words published in ephemeral journals are closer to after-dinner conversation than to literature, just as Doyle's adventure tales in dialogue (see the Appendix) are closer to verbal discourse than to written matter. The personal warmth of the spoken word gives the narrative a greater depth and urgency.

More than intermittently engaging the reader's attention, Holmes and Watson seem to demand a stronger response. A minority find the detective cold and mechanical, arrogant and uninteresting; the doctor simplistic and dull; and detective stories in general artificial and tedious. For the many, the characters and plots are interesting, the characters far more than the plots—as well constructed mysteries, two-thirds of the plots barely rate a passing grade.

On the one hand, a small but significant percentage of readers feel called upon to continue the stories into the present, to reconstruct untold tales, to search out lost documents, to comment upon events within and beyond the actual narratives, and to criticize the details, the logic, and chronology of Watson's records. On the other hand, a large number of persons who know many details of the Holmes canon have never actually read a word written by Doyle. Although the resulting picture may be somewhat distorted, a fairly recognizable composite of Holmes and Watson can be derived from a variety of alternative sources. This familiarity contributes to the confidence,

Conclusion: The Unified Field Theory of Detection

acceptance, and trust generated by the figures of the detective and the doctor.

Persons who have never read Cervantes may know the knight of the doleful countenance through many oblique references to his history. Don Quixote lives beyond the pages penned by Cervantes, tilting at more distant windmills, and is easily recognized in a Picasso sketch. The silhouettes of Holmes and Watson can be made out inching their blurred outlines through the thick London fog, solving the mysteries of existence by induction and deduction, observation and conjecture, innocence and luck. Their forms are the Kantian categories of the dreams of reason and imagination. They are among the shapes assumed by clouds of interstellar dust in the void between the destruction and creation of universes.

Do the great tales ever end? The great heroic tales of adventure filled journeys down fog-dimmed roads that go ever on, winding roads and sea-routes that—by detours and indirections, shipwrecks and lost trails that half rise to consciousness as clues to the meaning of the journey—always lead to the same journey's end—a cave or cottage of hobbit comforts, slippers by the rocking chair or nailed to the mantelpiece, the Ithaca from where it started. And where did the great tales begin, the great tales with heroes that had no birth?

Sherlock Holmes is an example of Merton's palimpsestic syndrome. Just as an epic will attribute the deeds of earlier heroes to the most recent champion, the world's most famous detective has been observed to assume and concentrate all the mythical reasoning powers of physicians and charlatans, figures of literature and the imagination: "even if a man has not actually done a given good thing," wrote Aristotle in his *Rhetoric*, "we shall bestow *praise* on him, if we are sure that he is the sort of man who *would* do it."[145] The magical cavern of 221 B Baker Street is a realm of shadows, Platonic shadows of all humanity's attempts to make sense of the mysterious universe, distorted shadows misshapen by the blinding light of Victorian optimism and its illusory faith in progress and perfectibility, eternal shadows of the highest human aspirations.

Appendix: Quantitative Stylistic Analysis of the Sixty Sherlock Holmes Stories and Selected Pastiches

> All things are numbers.
> —Pythagoras

> Were it not for number and its nature, nothing that exists would be clear to anybody either in itself or in its relation to other things.
> —Philolaus

> I cultivate a simple style and avoid long words so far as possible.
> —Doyle, " The Truth about Sherlock Holmes"

There are nine basic forms of speech: legend, saga, myth, riddle, proverb, case, memoir, tale, and joke. The Holmes canon exemplifies all these forms through an inspired manipulation of language. Commentaries focus on irrelevant clues that are more obvious in the period illustrations than in the letter of the text. There are very few actual facts in the Sherlock Holmes stories; what is really there are words about facts—client narratives, police misinterpretations, detective deductions, and medical comments. The analytic technique proper to the study of Sherlock Holmes is neither detection nor logic but rhetoric. Holmes does not represent a disembodied abstract dialectic but a flexible humanist application of the reasoning sense to unique cases. The ancients referred to this forensic grammar as rhetoric. The next generation of Sherlockian studies will need to be linguistic.

The following tables represent a preliminary attempt to apply mathematical analysis to the style of the original Sherlock Holmes stories and their imitators. The techniques are those of Rudolf Flesch ("A New Readability Yardstick," *Journal of Applied Psychology* 32 [1948]: 221–33).[146] Reading Ease (RE) is calculated from the formula:

$$RE = 206.835 - .846\, SYLL - 1.015\, SL,$$

where SL is the average sentence length in words and SYLL is the number of syllables per 100 words. Human Interest (HI) is calculated from the formula:

$$HI = 3.635\, PW + .314\, PS,$$

where PW is the number of personal words per 100 words and PS the number of personal sentences. Sampling procedures, as outlined by Flesch, were followed with the exception of PS, which was calculated on the same 100-word samples that were utilized for the other three indexes. The total number of words sampled was just over 175,000. A programmable TI-55 was used for all computations. At the extremes, low Reading Ease scores of 0 to 30 typify very difficult material, while high scores of 90 to 100 suggest very easy material. Low Human Interest scores of 0 to 10 indicate very dull and insipid writing, while scores in the 60 to 100 range characterize a very dramatic style.

Table I applies these formulas to Doyle's sixty Holmes narratives. In *A Study in Scarlet*, the Utah narrative of Jefferson Hope is written in an entirely different style with SL = 20.7 and PS = 38.8 and has, therefore, been excluded from the computations for that book. It is similar for the Scowrers flashback in *The Valley of Fear*, where the differences, although not striking, were consistent. The two tales purportedly authored by Holmes, "The Blanched Solider" and "The Lion's Mane," do not differ significantly from other tales in the Casebook; "The Musgrave Ritual," a tale verbally narrated by Holmes, does not differ significantly from the Memoirs or the remainder of the canon. Do the similar styles reflect similar mentalities or revisions by literary agents such as A. C. Doyle and A. P. Watt?

Table II applies the formulas to the longest series of Sherlockian pastiches (and probably the best), August Derleth's Solar Pons. One example of a second order imitation is included for comparison.

Table III mathematically analyzes the styles found in a wide cross-section of Holmesian literature.

One of the most striking results obtained from the Flesch formulas is the high percent of personal sentences (mostly direct quotations) in the Canon; few of the imitators come close. It is also interesting to note the Σ scores achieved by two works aimed at a children's audience: Newman's *Case of the Baker Street Irregulars* and Titus's *Basil of Baker Street*. The Holmes stories are themselves written at a ninth-grade level. The two volumes by Theodore Roosevelt are included for comparison with Jeffers's *Adventure of the Stalwart Companions*, purportedly (but obviously not) penned by T.R.

KEY TO STORY TITLES

ABBE	The Abbey Grange
BERY	The Beryl Coronet
BLAC	Black Peter
BLAN	The Blanched Soldier
BLUE	The Blue Carbuncle
BOSC	The Boscombe Valley Mystery
BRUC	The Bruce-Partington Plans
CARD	The Cardboard Box
CHAS	Charles Augustus Milverton
COPP	The Copper Beeches
CREE	The Creeping Man
CROO	The Crooked Man
DANC	The Dancing Men
DEVI	The Devil's Foot
DYIN	The Dying Detective
EMPT	The Empty House
ENGR	The Engineer's Thumb
FINA	The Final Problem
FIVE	The Five Orange Pips
GLOR	The "Gloria Scott"
GOLD	The Golden Pince-Nez
GREE	The Greek Interpreter
HOUN	The Hound of the Baskervilles
IDEN	A Case of Identity
ILLU	The Illustrious Client
LADY	The Disappearance of Lady Frances Carfax
LAST	His Last Bow
LION	The Lion's Mane
MAZA	The Mazarin Stone
MISS	The Missing Three-Quarter
MUSG	The Musgrave Ritual
NAVA	The Naval Treaty
NOBL	The Noble Bachelor

NORW	The Norwood Builder
PRIO	The Priory School
REDC	The Red Circle
REDH	The Red-headed League
REIG	The Reigate Squires
RESI	The Resident Patient
RETI	The Retired Colourman
SCAN	A Scandal in Bohemia
SECO	The Second Stain
SHOS	Shoscombe Old Place
SIGN	The Sign of Four
SILV	Silver Blaze
SIXN	The Six Napoleons
SOLI	The Solitary Cyclist
SPEC	The Speckled Band
STOC	The Stockbroker's Clerk
STUD	A Study in Scarlet
SUSS	The Sussex Vampire
THOR	The Problem of Thor Bridge
3GAB	The Three Gables
3GAR	The Three Garridebs
3STU	The Three Students
TWIS	The Man with the Twisted Lip
VALL	The Valley of Fear
VEIL	The Veiled Lodger
WIST	Wisteria Lodge
YELL	The Yellow Face

Table I

Sherlock Holmes (John J. Watson/Arthur C. Doyle)						
Title	SL	SYLL	RE	PW	PS	HI
Adventures (1892)						
SCAN	14.0	143.4	70	12.2	75.0	68.0
REDH	16.2	132.0	76	11.6	97.1	72.5
IDEN	20.0	138.6	67	13.4	85.7	75.6
BOSC	18.0	135.8	71	13.6	80.7	74.7
FIVE	14.0	130.2	80	17.0	100.0	93.2
TWIS	19.2	137.4	68	11.6	88.9	70.1
BLUE	15.0	131.6	77	10.8	94.4	68.9
SPEC	15.4	131.4	76	13.2	94.1	77.6
ENGR	17.4	130.6	76	16.6	100.0	91.7
NOBL	11.0	136.0	79	9.6	98.0	65.7
BERY	16.2	134.0	74	14.6	85.3	79.9
COPP	15.8	134.8	75	13.2	92.3	77.0
mean	16.0	134.7	74.1	13.1	91.0	76.2
σ	2.5	3.9	4.2	2.2	8.0	8.7
Memoirs (1894)						
SILV	24.0	145.8	57	8.2	81.0	55.2
YELL	14.4	127.6	81	16.4	92.3	88.6
STOC	17.0	138.2	70	10.6	70.6	60.7
GLOR	18.8	137.8	69	11.8	100.0	74.3
MUSG	16.2	130.0	77	13.6	90.6	77.9
REIG	18.0	140.4	67	12.2	66.7	65.3
CROO	17.6	132.6	74	12.8	100.0	77.9
RESI	18.0	145.6	63	10.0	90.9	64.9
GREE	14.2	133.4	78	13.8	97.3	80.7
NAVA	18.8	136.0	70	10.6	83.3	64.7
FINA	11.2	143.0	73	15.6	100.0	88.1
mean	17.1	137.3	70.8	12.3	88.4	72.6
σ	3.3	6.1	6.9	2.5	11.7	11.1
Return (1905)						
EMPT	23.2	141.8	60	10.8	70.4	61.4
NORW	18.8	130.6	74	12.2	77.8	68.8
DANC	16.2	138.6	71	12.8	71.4	68.9
SOLI	14.4	131.4	78	13.8	73.7	73.3
PRIO	16.0	143.4	67	8.8	83.3	58.2

Table I cont.

Title	SL	SYLL	RE	PW	PS	HI
Return (1905)						
BLAC	17.2	134.4	73	9.6	58.5	53.3
CHAS	15.0	137.0	74	11.2	57.1	58.6
SIXN	16.8	132.4	75	12.2	84.4	70.9
3STU	10.4	133.0	81	10.8	72.0	61.9
GOLD	13.0	132.6	79	9.4	92.7	63.3
MISS	16.8	138.6	70	14.6	74.5	76.5
ABBE	18.2	139.2	68	10.2	83.9	63.6
SECO	14.4	142.8	70	12.6	83.3	72.0
mean	16.2	136.6	72.3	11.5	75.6	65.4
σ	3.1	4.5	5.6	1.8	10.2	6.9
Last Bow (1917)						
WIST	11.6	133.8	80	13.4	95.8	78.8
CARD	13.6	143.8	70	11.2	95.1	70.6
REDC	10.4	136.2	79	12.6	88.2	73.5
BRUC	12.2	144.2	71	9.4	89.1	62.2
DYIN	12.2	137.8	76	14.0	66.7	71.8
LADY	13.8	134.0	76	14.8	81.0	79.2
DEVI	22.0	144.2	60	12.6	57.7	63.9
LAST	9.2	131.2	84	13.8	89.1	78.2
mean	13.1	138.2	74.5	12.7	82.8	72.3
σ	3.9	5.3	7.5	1.7	13.7	6.6
Casebook (1927)						
ILLU	13.8	131.0	79	17.8	100.0	96.1
BLAN	12.4	131.0	80	13.0	95.2	77.2
MAZA	9.8	132.6	82	12.0	79.3	68.5
3GAB	13.0	133.4	78	13.0	95.5	77.3
SUSS	15.2	139.2	71	14.2	77.8	76.0
3GAR	11.8	130.2	82	13.8	81.6	75.8
THOR	12.0	134.0	79	12.2	91.5	73.1
CREE	13.4	146.0	68	10.4	69.1	59.5
LION	10.2	131.4	83	10.8	82.7	65.3
VEIL	12.0	130.5	81	12.5	79.4	70.3
SHOS	9.4	131.8	83	12.8	74.6	69.9
RETI	13.6	142.2	71	11.6	92.5	71.3
mean	12.2	134.4	78.1	12.8	84.9	73.4
σ	1.8	5.2	5.2	1.9	9.7	8.9

Table I cont.

Title	SL	SYLL	RE	PW	PS	HI
STUD *1887*	14.5 *3.6**	140.2 *11.4*	71	13.7 *5.0*	82.6	75.7
SIGN *1890*	15.8 *4.0*	136.4 *10.4*	73	11.8 *3.6*	76.9	67.0
HOUN *1901-2*	15.4 *8.3*	135.0 *9.6*	74	11.7 *5.3*	89.7	70.7
VALL *1914-15*	15.2 *5.4*	140.5 *14.1*	70	11.7 *4.9*	78.0	67.0
Canon *all nine volumes*	15.1 *1.6*	137.0 *2.3*	73.1 *2.5*	12.4 *0.8*	83.3 *5.7*	71.1 *3.9*
Intro** *N=60*	30.2 *14.9*	150.3 *11.9*		8.7 *4.2*	19.5 *32.1*	

* For books, numbers in italics represent one standard deviation (σ).
Σ is an artificial index of comparison defined by the formula:
$\Sigma = RE + HI$. For all nine volumes Σ is 144.2.
** In Flesch's system introductions are always analyzed separately.

Table II

Solar Pons (August Derleth)						
Title	SL	SYLL	RE	PW	PS	HI
Regarding Sherlock Holmes						
FRIG	17.0	141.8	67	13.6	88.6	77.2
LATE	11.4	143.4	72	8.8	95.6	62.0
BLAN	13.8	155.2	61	10.6	69.1	60.2
NORC	18.6	144.2	64	14.6	86.2	80.2
RETI	16.8	146.0	64	12.2	82.4	70.3
3RED	12.0	143.2	72	9.2	59.5	52.1
SOTH	13.8	143.8	70	8.2	82.1	55.6
PURL	12.0	137.0	76	12.8	83.7	72.8
LIMP	17.6	145.0	64	13.8	84.9	76.9
7PAS	12.8	145.8	69	11.0	81.0	65.4
LAST	11.6	143.2	73	13.2	78.0	72.5
BROF	16.2	140.0	70	11.8	86.8	70.2
mean	14.5	144.1	68.5	11.7	81.5	68.0
σ	2.6	4.3	4.5	2.1	9.4	8.9
Chronicles						
REDL	10.8	143.4	73	11.6	92.3	71.2
ORIE	10.2	155.0	65	16.0	73.1	81.2
GOLD	11.6	144.0	72	13.6	95.5	79.4
SHAP	11.6	135.6	78	13.2	85.1	74.7
BENI	11.0	148.8	69	12.2	77.1	68.6
MIST	16.2	141.0	69	9.2	87.9	61.0
ALUM	11.8	141.4	74	10.8	80.4	64.6
7SIS	13.4	147.6	67	9.2	72.5	56.2
BISH	13.8	128.8	81	16.0	78.1	82.7
UNIQ	18.4	141.2	66	10.6	73.7	61.6
mean	12.9	142.7	71.4	12.2	81.6	70.1
σ	2.6	7.2	5.2	2.5	8.2	9.3
Memoirs						
CIRC	17.6	151.0	60	7.6	73.0	50.5
PERF	13.8	137.2	74	17.8	79.5	89.7
BROC	14.2	148.8	65	13.8	73.0	73.1
DOGM	10.2	141.0	75	9.2	63.4	53.3
PROP	11.6	144.0	72	14.0	81.3	76.4
RICO	15.2	159.2	56	10.2	97.6	67.8

Table II cont.

Title	SL	SYLL	RE	PW	PS	HI
Memoirs						
6SIL	18.3	147.3	61	10.0	34.8	47.3
LOSL	12.2	141.8	73	9.0	73.2	55.7
TOTT	18.2	149.2	60	9.0	60.6	51.7
5ROY	18.4	151.4	59	8.8	51.7	48.2
PARA	17.0	144.0	65	11.6	82.7	68.2
mean	15.2	146.8	65.5	11.0	70.1	62.0
σ	3.0	6.1	6.9	3.1	17.0	13.9
Casebook						
SUSS	9.8	135.6	80	14.0	70.9	73.2
HAUN	13.8	141.0	72	9.8	67.5	56.8
FATA	14.8	145.2	67	12.6	81.3	71.3
INTA	11.8	140.6	74	14.4	84.1	78.7
SPUR	13.0	142.6	71	13.0	81.0	72.7
CHIN	9.8	146.0	72	13.8	81.1	75.7
ASCO	12.0	133.0	80	15.8	93.9	86.9
CROU	19.2	151.6	57	9.4	73.3	57.2
MISH	14.0	144.6	69	11.8	73.2	65.9
AMAT	10.6	143.4	73	12.2	75.0	68.0
WHIS	11.0	142.2	74	11.0	77.6	64.4
INNK	21.2	135.0	67	8.4	73.5	53.6
mean	13.4	141.7	71.3	12.2	77.7	68.7
σ	3.6	5.2	6.2	2.2	7.1	9.8
Reminiscences						
MAZA	18.2	150.8	60	11.2	63.3	60.6
HATS	11.8	139.8	75	12.6	72.1	68.4
MOSA	11.6	147.2	69	11.8	78.7	67.6
PRAE	12.0	142.2	72	11.8	83.0	69.0
CLOV	14.0	132.4	78	13.0	80.5	72.6
BLAC	13.6	154.2	61	12.2	80.0	69.5
TROU	12.2	151.2	65	10.6	75.0	62.1
BLIN	13.4	136.4	75	15.0	88.4	82.3
mean	13.4	144.3	69.4	12.3	77.6	69.0
σ	2.2	7.8	6.8	1.3	7.6	6.7

Table II cont.

Title	SL	SYLL	RE	PW	PS	HI
Return						
LOSD	12.0	139.4	75	12.4	86.4	72.2
DEVI	13.4	138.2	74	11.4	62.5	61.0
DORR	14.0	145.0	68	12.6	73.2	68.8
TRIP	12.8	146.2	69	14.4	82.9	78.3
RYDB	12.4	140.2	69	13.0	85.7	74.2
GRIC	15.2	143.6	68	12.4	74.3	68.4
STON	14.0	140.4	72	9.6	89.7	63.1
REMA	14.6	151.8	62	7.2	50.0	41.9
PENN	15.8	141.6	69	11.6	85.7	69.1
TRAI	20.4	146.6	60	8.4	75.8	54.3
CAMB	14.2	144.6	68	12.2	70.7	66.6
LITT	18.4	138.6	68	8.6	64.7	51.6
SWED	15.8	144.0	67	10.8	75.0	62.9
mean	14.9	143.1	68.4	11.1	75.1	64.0
σ	2.4	3.9	4.1	2.1	11.4	10.0
Mr. Fairlie's Final Journey						
mean	14.4	139.6	72.0	11.4	77.4	65.7
σ	10.3	10.9		4.9		
All 7 Derleth volumes						
mean	14.1	143.2	69.5	11.7	77.3	66.8
σ	0.9	2.3	2.3	0.6	3.9	3.0
***Further Adventures* (Basil Cooper)**						
SHAF	9.4	145.6	73	10.0	74.0	59.6
DEFE	12.6	145.0	70	10.0	68.3	57.9
SURR	10.6	146.4	71	12.8	76.0	70.4
MISS	15.0	142.0	70	11.2	56.4	58.4
mean	11.9	144.8	71.0	11.0	68.7	61.6
σ	2.5	1.9	1.4	1.3	8.8	5.9
z*	−2.4	0.7	0.7	−1.2	−2.2	−1.7

*The z score measures the number of standard deviations by which a given mean deviates from a population mean. In this instance, the population means are the Flesch indices for Derleth's seven volumes of Solar Pons tales; all z scores in Table III (in italics) refer to the mean indices for the nine volume Holmes saga. The Σ for all seven Solar Pons volumes is 136.3, for the single Cooper volume is 132.6.

Table III	SL	SYLL	RE	PW	PS	HI	Σ
The Case of the Man Who Was Wanted Whitaker/Watson	28.2 *8.2*	142.6 *2.4*	54.0 *−7.6*	7.6 *−6.0*	77.3 *−1.1*	51.9 *−4.9*	105.9
The Adventure of the Unique "Hamlet" Starrett/Watson	18.6 *2.2*	150.2 *5.7*	60.0 *−5.2*	10.6 *−2.3*	87.9 *0.8*	66.1 *−1.3*	126.1
The Exploits of Sherlock Holmes Doyle/Carr/Watson	13.2 *−1.2*	142.4 *2.4*	71.1 *−0.8*	12.0 *−0.5*	79.6 *−0.7*	63.6 *−1.9*	134.7
Solar Pons Derleth	14.1 *−0.6*	143.2 *2.7*	69.5 *−1.4*	11.7 *−0.9*	77.3 *−1.1*	66.8 *−1.1*	136.3
The Seven-Per-Cent Solution Meyer/Watson	18.3 *2.0*	146.1 *4.0*	62.0 *−4.4*	12.4 *0.0*	48.4 *−6.1*	60.3 *−2.8*	122.3
The West End Horror Meyer/Watson	13.3 *−1.1*	147.8 *4.7*	67.0 *−2.4*	11.4 *−1.3*	70.8 *−2.3*	63.6 *−1.9*	130.6
Sherlock Holmes's War of the Worlds Wellman/Wellman/Watson	14.7 *−0.3*	146.6 *4.2*	66.0 *−2.8*	9.7 *−3.4*	68.6 *−2.6*	56.8 *−3.7*	122.8
The Case of the Philosopher's Ring Collins/Watson	13.5 *−1.0*	143.8 *3.0*	70.0 *−1.2*	10.5 *−2.4*	76.9 *−1.1*	62.4 *−2.2*	132.4
Exit Sherlock Holmes Hall/Watson	16.2 *0.7*	143.0 *2.6*	67.0 *−2.4*	11.6 *−1.0*	41.0 *−7.4*	55.1 *−4.1*	122.1
The Last Sherlock Holmes Story Dibdin/Watson	14.2 *−0.6*	146.3 *4.0*	66.0 *−2.8*	10.4 *−2.5*	58.8 *−4.3*	56.3 *−3.8*	122.3
Sherlock Holmes versus Dracula Estleman/Watson	15.3 *0.1*	140.4 *1.5*	70.0 *−1.2*	11.8 *−0.8*	62.6 *−3.6*	62.6 *−2.2*	132.6
Dr. Jekyll and Mr. Holmes Estleman/Watson	17.4 *1.4*	145.0 *3.5*	64.0 *−3.6*	13.0 *0.8*	67.7 *−2.7*	68.6 *−0.6*	132.6
Sherlock Holmes and the Golden Bird Thomas/Watson	14.5 *−0.4*	146.1 *4.0*	67.0 *−2.4*	11.0 *−1.8*	55.0 *−5.0*	57.3 *−3.5*	124.3

Table III cont.

	SL	SYLL	RE	PW	PS	HI	Σ
Sherlock Holmes and the Sacred Sword	16.1	139.8	70.0	10.2	58.1	55.3	125.3
Thomas/Watson	0.6	1.2	−1.2	−2.8	−4.4	−4.1	
Adventure of the Peerless Peer	14.9	144.3	54.2	10.8	54.2	56.3	110.4
Farmer/Watson	−0.1	3.2	−7.6	−2.0	−5.1	−3.8	
Sherlock Holmes in New York	18.6	141.8	65.0	10.9	57.1	57.5	122.5
Benson/Watson	2.2	2.1	−3.2	−1.9	−4.6	−3.5	
Enter the Lion	13.6	143.5	70.0	13.1	65.4	68.1	138.1
Hodel/Wright/Mycroft	−0.9	2.8	−1.2	0.9	−3.1	−0.8	
Revenge of Moriarity	16.6	144.3	65.0	9.4	43.6	47.9	112.9
Gardner/Moriarity	1.0	3.2	−3.2	−3.8	−7.0	−6.0	
Return of Moriarity	20.8	143.2	61.0	9.2	48.0	48.5	109.5
Gardner/Moriarity	3.6	2.7	−4.8	−4.0	−6.2	−5.8	
Demon Device	19.0	159.7	51.0	10.6	41.1	51.4	102.4
Saffron/Doyle	2.4	2.4	−8.8	−2.3	−7.4	−5.1	
A Taste for Honey	17.6	138.0	70.0	11.8	51.3	59.0	129.0
Heard/Silchester	1.6	0.4	−1.2	−0.8	−5.6	−3.1	
Reply Paid	17.5	141.0	67.0	12.4	58.5	63.5	130.5
Heard/Silchester	1.5	1.7	−2.4	0.0	−4.4	−2.0	
The Notched Hairpin	25.6	138.1	60.0	11.7	64.2	62.7	122.7
Heard/Silchester	6.6	0.5	−5.2	−0.9	−3.4	−2.2	
Sherlock Holmes in Modern Times	21.4	145.0	60.0	10.2	69.9	59.1	119.1
Dworkin	3.9	3.5	−5.2	−2.8	−2.4	−3.1	
The Infernal Device	12.0	144.8	71.0	10.8	78.3	63.9	134.9
Kurland	−1.9	3.4	−0.8	−2.0	−0.9	−1.9	
The Adventure of Sherlock Holmes' Smarter Brother	12.0	149.7	67.0	11.4	54.3	58.5	125.5
Pearlman	−1.9	5.5	−2.4	−1.3	−5.1	−3.2	
Sherlock Holmes in Dallas	17.8	154.5	57.4	14.3	68.6	63.4	120.8
Aubrey/Watson	1.7	7.6	−6.3	2.4	−2.6	−2.0	

Table III cont.

	SL	SYLL	RE	PW	PS	HI	Σ
They Might be Giants Goldman	9.2 −3.7	142.1 2.2	75.0 0.8	12.5 0.1	69.3 −2.5	67.2 −1.0	142.2
The Adventure of the Stalwart Companions Jeffers/Roosevelt	18.8 2.3	147.5 4.6	69.0 −1.6	11.3 −1.4	88.0 0.8	68.7 −0.6	137.7
Rough Riders Roosevelt	26.6	148.0	52.0	8.7	5.2	33.2	85.2
Naval War of 1812 Roosevelt	27.7	158.7	43.0	3.3	4.8	13.5	56.5
Case of the Baker Street Irregulars Newman	11.7 −2.1	135.1 −0.8	78.0 2.0	14.0 2.0	77.4 −1.0	75.2 1.1	153.2
Basil of Baker Street Titus	10.2 −3.1	138.9 0.8	77.0 1.6	13.2 1.0	51.5 −5.6	64.2 −1.8	141.2
The Adventures of Creighton Holmes Hubbell	15.1 0.0	136.4 −0.3	73.7 0.2	12.2 −0.3	83.6 −0.1	70.7 −0.1	144.4
The Woman in Red Preiss/Reese	8.8 −3.9	140.8 1.7	76.0 1.2	16.2 4.8	93.2 1.7	88.2 4.4	164.2
A Three-Pipe Problem Symons	12.1 −1.9	139.1 0.9	75.0 0.8	11.7 −0.9	61.1 −3.9	61.7 −2.4	136.7
Watson's Choice Mitchell	16.1 0.6	143.5 2.8	66.0 −2.8	10.8 −2.0	70.5 −2.3	61.4 −2.5	127.4

Notes

1. Adapted from R. Barthes, *Image-Music-Text* (New York: Hill and Wang, 1977).
2. *Kalevala: The Land of the Heroes*, trans. W. F. Kirby (New York: E. P. Dutton and Company, 1961), vol. 1, runo 3, lines 13–14, p. 20.
3. Robert Jay Lifton, *Boundaries: Psychological Man in Revolution* (New York: Random House, 1969), p. xi.
4. C. M. Bowra, *From Virgil to Milton* (London: Macmillan, 1957), p. 9.
5. W. P. Ker, *Epic and Romance: Essays on Medieval Literature* (London: Macmillan, 1922).
6. Nemours H. Clement, *The Influence of the Arthurian Romances on the Five Books of Rabelais* (New York: Phaeton Press, 1970), pp. 176–205.
7. Bradford B. Broughton's *The Legends of King Richard I Coeur De Lion: A Study of Sources and Variations to the Year 1600* (The Hague: Mouton and Company, 1966) illustrates the attachment of myths to this historic personage. The relevant texts are translated in the same author's *Richard the Lion-Hearted and Other Medieval English Romances* (New York: E. P. Dutton and Company, 1966). In a similar vein, Kingsley Amis in *The James Bond Dossier* (New York: New American Library, 1965) shows how a literary character may achieve a popular interpretation totally at odds with the written text.
8. S. H. Holbrook, *The Golden Age of Quackery* (New York: Collier, 1962), p. 130.
9. Guglielmo Ferrero, *The Gamble: Bonaparte in Italy 1796–1797* (New York: Walker and Company, 1961), p. 19.
10. Albert Leon Guérard, *Reflections on the Napoleonic Legend* (New York: Charles Scribner's Sons, 1924), pp. 180–81.
11. The use of skepticism to euhemerize (debunk) Napoleonic fact was first attempted by Archbishop Richard Whately's *Historic Doubts Relative to Napoleon Buonaparte* (1819), reprinted in Houston Peterson, ed., *Essays in Philosophy* (New York: Pocket Library, 1959), pp. 143–71.
12. In his *Curious Myths of Middle Ages* (1866–68; repr. New Hyde Park, N.Y.: University Books, 1967), Sabine Baring-Gould quotes the reduction of Napoleon to a solar myth (pp. 127–33).
13. Mark R. Hillegas, *The Future as Nightmare: H. G. Wells and the Anti-Utopians* (New York: Oxford University Press, 1967).
14. Although it would go well beyond the limited scope of this brief monograph, one of the most important topics for future Sherlock Holmes scholarship is the contribution of classical rhetorical devices to the structure of the canon. Biographical material on Conan Doyle confirms his familiarity with all the relevant major literary models. A perusal of chapters 8 and 9 of Ernst

Robert Curtius, *European Literature and the Latin Middle Ages* (Princeton: Princeton University Press, 1953), will suggest the potential yield from investigations in this area, and the renaissance in the study of rhetoric over the past decade has made available the requisite technical expertise.

15. The most comprehensive recent biography of Conan Doyle is Charles Higham, *The Adventures of Conan Doyle: The Life of the Creator of Sherlock Holmes* (New York: Pocket Books, 1978).

16. Quoted in Charles Snyder, "There's Money in Ears, But the Eye Is a Gold Mine," *Archives of Ophthalmology* 85 (March 1971): 365.

17. A recent reprinting of the Brigadier Gerard stories has had the Sherlockian passion for chronology applied to the text with dates and ages rectified to convert fiction to pseudohistory. The reductio ad absurdum of this misguided methodology is easily imagined (if it has not already been reached) when one considers the possible result of amending literary classics to conform to such a corrected chronology. Temporal sequences play an exceedingly important role in such works as Dante's *Comedia* and Joyce's *Ulysses*, but the frames of reference are as much internal as external.

18. The mythical Lane's disease is described in Edward C. Lambert, *Modern Medical Mistakes* (Bloomington: Indiana University Press, 1978), pp. 15–22.

19. W. W. Rowe, *Dostoevsky: Child and Man in His Works* (New York: New York University Press, 1968), p. 144.

20. Martin Gardner, "The Irrelevance of Conan Doyle," in Michael Harrison, ed., *Beyond Baker Street* (Indianapolis, Ind.: Bobbs-Merrill, 1976), pp. 123–35.

21. Quoted in H. Douglas Thomson, *Masters of Mystery: A Study of the Detective Story* (New York: Dover, 1978), p. 125.

22. Quoted in Edward E. Harnagel, "Joseph Bell, M.D.—the Real Sherlock Holmes," *The New England Journal of Medicine* 258 (5 June 1958): 1158.

23. Conan Doyle, *Memories and Adventures* (1924), quoted in E. P. Scarlett, "The Method of Zadig," *Archives of Internal Medicine* 117 (June 1966): 833.

24. C.C. Stisted quoted in Irving Wallace, "The Incredible Dr. Bell," *Saturday Review of Literature* 31 (1948): 7–8.

25. Conan Doyle, quoted in Thomson, *Masters of Mystery*, p. 126.

26. Joseph Bell, quoted in Joseph V. Klauder, "Sherlock Holmes as a Dermatologist," *A.M.A. Archives of Dermatology and Syphilology* 68 (October 1953): 363. A compendium of modern occupational signs and diagnoses is E. R. Plunkett, *Folk Name & Trade Diseases* (Stamford, Conn.: Barrett Book Co., 1978). A selection from this work appears in Paul Trachtman, "Monday Head to Tango Foot (and Worse), It's Sick, Sick, Sick," *Smithsonian*, April 1979, pp. 123–34.

27. Quoted in Thompson, *Masters of Mystery*, p. 125.

28. Quoted in John Dickson Carr, *The Life of Sir Arthur Conan Doyle* (New York: Vintage, 1975), p. 35.

29. Arthur Conan Doyle, preface to *A Study in Scarlet* (London: Ward Lock and Bowden, 1894).

30. Joseph Bell, quoted in Vincent Starrett, *The Private Life of Sherlock Holmes* (New York: Pinnacle Books, 1975), p. 21.

31. Zeta (Z.C.), *The Diagnosis of the Acute Abdomen in Rhyme* (London: H. K. Lewis & Co. Ltd., 1962), p. 5.

32. A. R. G. Owen, *Hysteria, Hypnosis and Healing: The Work of Jean-Martin Charcot* (New York: Garrett, 1971), p. 36.

33. Quoted in Harnagel, "Joseph Bell, M.D.—the Real Sherlock Holmes," p. 1159.

34. Quoted in ibid., p. 1159.

35. The major primary surce of biographical data on Dr. Holmes is John T. Morse, Jr., *Life and Letters of Oliver Wendell Holmes*, 2 vols. (Boston: Houghton, Mifflin and Company, 1897).

36. N. P. Willis, quoted in M. A. DeWolfe Howe, *Holmes of the Breakfast Table* (New York: Oxford University Press, 1939), p. 95.

37. O. W. Holmes, quoted in Eleanor M. Tilton, *Amiable Autocrat: A Biography of Dr. Oliver Wendell Holmes* (New York: Henry Schuman, 1947), p. 138.

38. Oliver Wendell Holmes, *Medical Essays 1842–1882* (Boston: Houghton Mifflin Co., 1911), p. 389.

39. Oliver Wendell Holmes, *The Autocrat of the Breakfast Table* (Boston: Houghton Mifflin and Company, 1889), 1:13.

40. Oliver Wendell Holmes, *Over the Teacups* (Boston: Houghton Mifflin Co., 1918), p. 129.

41. Holmes, *The Autocrat of the Breakfast Table*, vol. 1, p. 6.

42. Holmes, *Medical Essays 1842–1882*, p. 211.

43. That the American doctor had a clergyman father and that much of his philosophy of life was in direct opposition to his father's faith were facts whose significance could not have been lost on Doyle. The name Holmes may also reflect some dim association with Sterne's clergyman, Dr. Homenas in *Tristram Shandy*, or even Rabelais's Homenas, the bishop of the Papimanes.

44. Dr. Milner Fothergill's story is quoted in Sir Lauder Brunton's retelling by Scarlett, "The Method of Zadig," pp. 832–35.

45. The association between the trick of observing and deducing details of a client's life and the fine art of medical quackery is of great antiquity. In the Arabic tale of "The Weaver Who Became a Leach", a henpecked husband takes up as a physician and is observed by the great healer Jalinus (Galen):

> Presently, up came a woman, and when the Weaver saw her afar off, he said to her, "Is not your husband a Jew and is not his ailment flatulence?" "Yes," replied the woman, and the folk marveled at this; wherefore the man was magnified in the eyes of Jalinus, for that *he heard speech such as was not of the usage of doctors*. Then the woman asked, "What is the remedy?" and the Weaver answered, "Bring the honorarium." So she paid him a dirham and he gave her medicines contrary to that ailment and such as would only aggravate the complaint. [italics added]

Challenged by Jalinus to explain his performance, the Weaver replies,

> "We people of Persia are skilled in physiognomy, and I saw the woman to be rosy-cheeked, blue-eyed, and tall-statured. These qualities belong not to the women of Roum; moreover, I saw her burning with anxiety; so I knew that the patient was her husband. As for his strangerhood, I noted that the dress of the woman differed from that of the townsfolk, wherefore I knew that she was a foreigner; and in her hand I saw a yellow rag, which garred me wot that the sick man was a Jew and she a Jewess. Moreover, she came to me on First Day; and 'tis the Jew's custom to take meat-puddings and food that hath passed the night and eat them on the Saturday their Sabbath, hot and cold, and they exceed in eating; wherefore flatulence and indigestion betide them. Thus I was directed and guessed that which thou hast heard."

A similar tale from the Turkish of Ahmed Ibn Hemdem She Ketk-Hoda (called Sohailee) relates the encounter between "Avicenna and the Observant Young Man." The greatest of Arabic physicians observes a young man distributing remedies in the marketplace. The latter again diagnoses a Jewess but also uncovers the identity of the incognito court healer. The Weaver story is found in Julian Hawthorne, ed., *Library of the World's Best Mystery and Detective Stories* (New York: Review of Reviews, 1908), 6: 45–49.

46. Samuel Tenenbaum, "Chelm's Doctor," *The Wise Men of Chelm* (New York: Collier, 1969), pp. 38–45.

47. Samuel Tenenbaum, "It Figures," *The Wise Men of Chelm*, pp. 153–54.

48. J. W. Courtney, "Dr. Watson and Mr. Holmes; or the Worm That Turned," *Boston Medical and Surgical Journal* 150 (26 May 1904): 553–55.

49. William Osler, *Aequanimitas with Other Addresses* (Philadelphia: P. Blakiston's Son and Company, 1928), pp. 348–49.

50. All quotations from Poe are taken from *The Best Known Works of Edgar Allan Poe* (8 vols.) with a biographical introduction by Hervey Allen (New York: Blue Ribbon Books, 1927). The four tales of detection are located in volume 2: "The Gold Bug" (GB), pp. 53–78; "The Murders in the Rue Morgue" (RM), pp. 78–103; "The Mystery of Marie Roget" (MR), pp. 103–38; and "The Purloined Letter" (PL), pp. 138–51.

51. As a cryptographer, Poe comes off rather poorly compared with Doyle in David Kahn, *The Codebreakers: The Story of Secret Writing* (New York: Macmillan, 1967), p. 785.

52. Dorothy Sayers, quoted in Thomson, *Masters of Mystery*, p. 83.

53. John Walsh, *Poe the Detective: The Curious Circumstances behind the Mystery of Marie Roget* (New Brunswick, N.J.: Rutgers University Press, 1968), p. 93. This work thoroughly deflates Poe's pretensions to any real-life detective skills.

54. *The Best Known Works of Edgar Allan Poe*, 8:813.

55. Thomson, *Masters of Mystery*, pp. 93–108.

56. Ian Ousby, *Bloodhounds of Heaven: The Detective in English Fiction from Godwin to Doyle* (Cambridge: Harvard University Press, 1976), p. 55. See also Samuel Edwards, *The Vidocq Dossier: The Story of the World's First Detective* (Boston: Houghton Mifflin, 1977).

57. This translation of the detective passages in *Vicomte de Bragelonne* is taken from *World's Greatest Detective Stories*, 10 vols. (New York: Walter J. Black, Inc., 1928), 2: 179–81. In her introduction to the first *Omnibus of Crime* (New York: Payson & Clarke, 1929), Dorothy Sayers attributes the famous tracking passages in the *Vicomte de Bragelonne* to the literary influence of James Fenimore Cooper's *Leatherstocking Tales*.

58. Miguel de Cervantes Saavedra, *El Ingenioso Hidalgo Don Quixote de la Mancha* (Madrid: Espasa-Calpe, S. A., 1970), p. 672.

59. François Marie Arouet de Voltaire, "Zadig the Babylonian," trans. in Julian Hawthorne, ed., *Library of the World's Best Mystery and Detective Stories: French, Italian, Spanish, Latin* (New York: Review of Reviews, 1908), pp. 208–9 (complete text, pp. 201–59). Irving Babbitt edited the French text (Boston: D. C. Heath & Co., 1905).

60. Ludwig Edelstein, "Sydenham and Cervantes," *Ancient Medicine*, ed. O. and C. L. Temkin (Baltimore: Johns Hopkins Press, 1967), pp. 455–61. This essay is an unsatisfactory reflection on Sydenham's famous advice to Sir Richard Blackmore.

61. Miguel de Cervantes, *The Adventures of Don Quixote* (New York: Dodd, Mead & Company, 1962). All the quotations from *Don Quixote* are from this edition except those marked with a "P"; these latter quotations from the novel are taken instead from a critical work by R. L. Predmore, *The World of Don Quixote* (Cambridge: Harvard University Press, 1967) in which the extensive quotations differ from extant translations. Thus, all citations have first a part number and then a chapter number, while those from Predmore have an additional page number.

62. Francisco Navarro Ledesma, *Cervantes: The Man and His Genius* (New York: Charterhouse, 1973), p. 325.

63. Miguel de Unamuno, *Our Lord Don Quixote: The Life of Don Quixote and Sancho with Sixteen Essays*, trans. Anthony Kerrigan (Princeton: Princeton University Press, 1967), p. 322.

64. Richard Sterne, *John Gielgud Directs Richard Burton in Hamlet: A Journal of Rehearsals* (New York: Random House, 1967) documents the background to that production. There is an early German version of *Hamlet, Bestrafte Brudermord* ("Fratricide Punished"), that in its stripped-down plot is more recognizable as a story of detection. See Aaron Marc Stein, "The Mystery Story in Cultural Perspective," in John Ball, ed., *The Mystery Story* (San Diego: University of California, 1976), pp. 28–59.

65. Giorgio de Santillana and Hertha von Dechend's *Hamlet's Mill: An Essay on Myth and the Frame of Time* (Boston: Gambit, 1969), pp. 12–18, researches Sherlock Holmes's debt to

Saxo Grammaticus. All the quotations from Saxo are taken from the de Santillana and von Dechend modification of Oliver Elton, *The First Nine Books of the History of Saxo Grammaticus* (London: Folk-Lore Society Publication 33, n.d.).

66. P. J. Chelkowski, *Mirror of the Invisible World: Tales from the Khamseh of Nizami* (New York: Metropolitan Museum of Art, 1975). This text contains an abridgement of "The Seven Princesses" (1197), a work with many similarities to (and differences from) its sixteenth-century Italian descendant.

The grandfather and grandmother of all story collections, *The Book of a Thousand Nights and a Night*, has often been indicated as the penultimate source of the tale of the three princes. Two of its many narratives reveal striking similarities, but in a much abbreviated and stripped-down form. In "The Sultan and His Three Sons," the three princes cannot agree to abide the division of their inheritance and go in search of an arbiter. They become charged with the theft of a camel that they describe (from its tracks and traces) in great detail but are then exonerated (à la Zadig the Babylonian). They then further demonstrate their brilliance by deducing the pedigree of their meal and their host Sultan—revealed to be the son of a cook. In "The Craft of the Three Sharpers" the tricksters' principal skill is the ability to deduce a genealogy from superficial details. They discover the pedigree of a colt by the shape of its hoof, of the queen by the proportions of her eyes, of the Sultan by his tendency to reward with food—he is again, of course, son of that ubiquitous cook. If genealogy (namely, genetics) is viewed as a branch of primitive medical knowledge, then these protophysicians make their fortune by their diagnostic skills.

Lest the multiplication of source materials in the present volume suggest an impossibly diffuse origin for the Holmes saga, it must be remembered that many of the classic collections of tales—*Somadeva* (Sanskrit), *Kah-Gyur* (Tibetan), *Pu Sung Ling* (Chinese), *Kikuchi Jun* (Japanese), Sa'di's *Būstān* (Persian), *Gesta Romanorum* (Latin), the Queen of Navarre's *Heptameron* and La Fontaine's *Contes* (French), Chaucer's *Canterbury Tales* (English), Boccaccio's *Decameron* (Italian)—and other ancient stories such as Daniel's matching wits with the priests of Bel as narrated in the fourteenth chapter of that prophetic book—all these exhibit not a trace of Sherlockian detective skills.

67. T. G. Remer, ed., *Serendipity and the Three Princes: From the Peregrinaggio of 1557* (Norman: University of Oklahoma Press, 1965), p. 6.

68. Modified from J. H. Austin, *Chase, Chance and Creativity: The Lucky Art of Novelty* (New York: Columbia University Press, 1978), p. 78.

69. John Stuart Mill, *Philosophy of Scientific Method*, ed. Ernest Nagel (New York: Hafner Publishing Co., 1950), p. 186.

70. Thomas A. Sebeok and Jean Umiker-Sebeok, *"You Know My Method:" A Juxtaposition of Charles S. Peirce and Sherlock Holmes* (Bloomington, Ind.: Gaslight, 1980).

71. L. G. Whitbread, trans., *Fulgentius the Mythographer* (Columbus: Ohio State University Press, 1971), pp. 84–85.

72. Jean Cocteau, "The Infernal Machine," trans. Albert Bermel in *The Infernal Machine and Other Plays* (New York: New Directions, 1963), p. 43. Cocteau's *la machine infernale* reappears in the two Sherlockian tales—Michael Kurland, *The Infernal Device* (New York: Signet, 1979) and Robert Saffron, *The Demon Device* (New York: Putnam, 1979).

73. Bernard Shaw, *The Millionairess* (Baltimore: Penguin Books, 1961), p. 27.

74. José Ortega y Gasset, *Meditations on Hunting* trans. H. B. Wescott, (New York: Charles Scribner's Sons, 1972), p. 53.

75. Ibid., p. 57.
76. Ibid., p. 59.
77. Ibid., p. 75.
78. Ibid., p. 142.

79. Francis Bacon, Preface to the *Instauratio Magna*, in *Prefaces and Prologues to Famous Books* (Harvard Classics, vol. 39; New York: P. F. Collier and Son, 1910), p. 140.

80. Francis Bacon, Epistle Dedicatory to the *Instauratio Magna* in *Prefaces and Prologues to Famous Books*, p. 120.

81. Quoted in William Irvine, *Apes, Angels, and Victorians* (New York: Meridian, 1959), p. 29.

82. Bernard Shaw, *Back to Methuselah: A Metabiological Pentateuch* (Baltimore: Penguin Books, 1961), p. 36.

83. Charles Darwin, *Origin of the Species*, quoted in Arthur Koestler, *The Act of Creation* (New York: Dell, 1973), p. 134.

84. Irvine, *Apes, Angels, and Victorians*, p. 83.

85. Howard E. Gruber and Paul H. Barrett, *Darwin on Man: A Psychological Study of Scientific Creativity Together with Darwin's Early and Unpublished Notebooks* (New York: E. P. Dutton & Co., 1974).

86. Charles Darwin, *Autobiography* (London: Watts & Co., 1949), p. 74.

87. H. G. Wells, *The Food of the Gods*, in *Seven Science Fiction Novels of H. G. Wells* (New York: Dover, n.d.), p. 634.

88. Marjorie Nicolson's 1929 essay "The Professor and the Detective" (reprinted in Howard Haycraft's classic anthology, *The Art of the Mystery Story: A Collection of Critical Essays* [New York: Simon and Schuster, 1946], pp. 110–27) specifically contrasts the Baconian method of Scotland Yard with the intuitive method of French detective bureaus. The English investigator "may laboriously and carefully accumulate all possible clues, passing over nothing as too insignificant, filling his little boxes and envelopes with all that comes his way, making no hypothesis, anticipating no conclusion, believing the man innocent until he can prove him guilty. Here he finds a single thread, there a grain of rice dropped in a drawing room; here he measures a footprint, there he photographs a thumb mark. His loot finally collected, he of Scotland Yard will select the 'dominant clue,' and that he will follow with grim persistence until the end." The intuitive continental ignores such clues to devote himself to thought. "Having, like his great predecessor, thought away all else in the universe, nothing remains but the culprit. By strength of logic alone, he has reconstituted the universe, and in his proper place has set the villain of the piece" (p. 126).

89. Quoted in Edward Kasner and James Newman, *Mathematics and the Imagination* (New York: Simon & Schuster, 1963), pp. 252–53.

90. Mill, *Philosophy of Scientific Method*, p. 203.

91. Henri Poincaré, *Science and Method* (New York: Dover, n.d.), p. 32.

92. Ibid., p. 28.

93. Ibid., p. 47. In his *aha! Insight* (San Francisco: W. H. Freeman, 1978), p. 98, Martin Gardner uses "The Problem of Thor Bridge" to distinguish the two stages in the solution of a scientific problem: a hypothesis generated by intuition or insight (the discovery process) is then tested by looking for deduced consequences of the proposed theory (logic of verification). The Zen *satori* may go back to the Sanscrit *aprthagyatnanirvartyaḥ* and *āśrayaparāvṛtti*: see J. M. Masson, introduction to W. S. Merwin and J. M. Masson, *Sanscrit Love Poetry* (New York: Columbia University Press, 1977), pp. 6, 18.

94. Adapted from J. C. Wright and Alice G. Vlietstra, "The Development of Selective Attention: From Perceptual Exploration to Logical Search," in H. Reese, ed., *Advances in Child Development and Behavior*, (New York: Academic Press, 1975), 10:194–239. See also Max Wertheimer, *Productive Thinking* (Chicago: University of Chicago Press, 1982).

95. Francis Bacon, *Novum Organum*, cxxii, quoted in Augustus de Morgan, *A Budget of Paradoxes*, 2d ed., ed. David Eugene Smith, (Chicago: Open Court, 1915), 1:77.

96. John Stuart Mill, quoted in Robert K. Merton, *On the Shoulders of Giants: A Shandean Postscript* (New York: Free Press, 1965), p. 261.

97. G. K. Chesterton, *The Father Brown Omnibus* (New York: Dodd, Mead & Company, 1951), p. 896.

98. G. K. Chesterton, *The Ball and the Cross* (Philadelphia: Dufour Editions, 1963), p. 71.

99. G. K. Chesterton, *The Club of Queer Trades* (Beaconsfield, Eng.: Darwen Finlayson, 1964), pp. 39–40, 22.

100. Chesterton, *The Father Brown Omnibus*, p. 107.

101. Ibid., p. 411.

102. Ibid., p. 639.

103. Quoted in David Stuart Davies, *Holmes of the Movies: The Screen Career of Sherlock Holmes* (New York: Bramhall House, 1976), p. 61. The addition of visual images to a written text ranges across a continuum: medieval and Renaissance illuminated manuscripts lie at one end of a spectrum that includes comic books at the other extreme. The use of line drawings and engravings to illustrate the early publications of many great works of fiction was a process frequently supervised by the authors as an integral part of their storytelling technique. Literary critics (including Marshall McLuhan) have scrupulously avoided analyzing the resulting psychological interaction (complex from the perspectives of both the artist and the audience), just as academic art critics have been at great pains to deny any narrative function to the visual arts. Although the iconographic representation of the great detective has been touched on in several publications—including B. Blackbeard, "Dealings with the Firm of Calabash, Deerstalker, and Lens: The Image of Sherlock Holmes in Popular Art and Literature," *Sherlock Holmes in America* (New York: Harry N. Abrams, 1981) and W. Klinefelter, *Sherlock Holmes in Portrait and Profile* (New York: Schocken Books, 1975)—there has not yet been constructed any general theory on the interaction between text and illustrations in great literature. Indeed, there is almost a presumption that the presence of illustrations rules out great literature or at the least raises some doubts about the critical faculties of the reader. When a theory of media interaction is attempted, it will need to take into account the retroactive influence on literature of later film and television productions. In recent decades, a number of volumes have collected and reprinted previously despised book illustrations from various sources, but the psychology of such art has too often been presumed to be a marketing one. That such artwork may reflect a visual icon of the reader's critical awareness has not yet been explored.

104. G. K. Chesterton, *The Paradoxes of Mr. Pond* (London: Darwen Finlayson, 1963), p. 63.

105. G. K. Chesterton, *A Miscellany of Men* (New York: Dodd, Mead and Co., 1912), p. 283.

106. Chesterton, *The Father Brown Omnibus*, p. 846.

107. Ibid., p. 63.

108. Lynette Hunter, *G. K. Chesterton: Explorations in Allegory* (New York: St. Martin's Press, 1979), p. 155.

109. Chesterton, *A Miscellany of Men*, p. 279.

110. Chesterton, *The Father Brown Omnibus*, p. 24.

111. G. K. Chesterton, *A Handful of Authors* (New York: Sheed and Ward, 1953), p. 168.

112. G. K. Chesterton, *Charles Dickens* (London: Methuen & Co., 1906), p. 65.

113. The classic example of "originology" is Erik H. Erickson's *Gandhi's Truth: On the Origins of Militant Nonviolence* (New York: W. W. Norton & Co., 1969). This fallacy, the opposite of teleology, is exploded in Jaques Barzun, *Darwin, Marx, Wagner: Critique of a Heritage* (Garden City, N.Y.: Anchor, 1958), pp. 51, 314.

114. William W. Ireland's classic in neuropsychology (first published in 1886), *The Blot upon the Brain* (Freeport: Books for Libraries Press, 1972), p. 289, cites a Dublin monograph, "Consideration of the Structural and Acquisitional Elements in Dextral Pre-eminence, with Conclusions as to the Ambidexterity of Primeval Man," by George Sigerson, M.D. It should be noted that there was no real need for Doyle to resurrect Sherlock Holmes in order to chronicle other (earlier) adventures—a tactic that he actually employed. The death, hiatus, and return of Holmes had the effect, among others, of turning the later tales into parafiction, into commentary on the earlier stories, much as "The Empty House" is a rewriting/rereading/reworking of "The Final Problem." David Grossvogel in *Mystery and Its Fictions: From Oedipus to Agatha*

Christie (Baltimore: Johns Hopkins University Press, 1979) suggests this in his discussion of Jorge Luis Borges's "Pierre Menard, Author of the Quixote" (pp. 136–37).

115. Peter L. Brown, *Comets, Meteorites and Men* (New York: Taplinger Publishing Co., 1973).

116. Adapted from G. J. Clifford, *The Shape of American Education* (Englewood-Cliffs, N.J.: Prentice-Hall, 1975), E. Friedson, *The Profession of Medicine: A Study of the Sociology of Applied Knowledge* (New York: Dodd, Mead Co., 1975), and S. H. King, *Perception of Illness and Medical Practice* (New York: Russell Sage Foundation, 1962).

117. Charles Baudelaire, *Flowers of Evil and Other Works*, ed. Wallace Fowlie (New York: Bantam, 1964), pp. 192–207. See also John Middleton Murray in Henri Peyre, ed., *Baudelaire: A Collection of Critical Essays* (Englewood Cliffs, N.J.: Prentice-Hall, 1962), p. 96.

118. *Selected Writings of Thomas de Quincey*, ed. Philip van Doren Stern (New York: Random House, 1957), "On Murder Considered as One of the Fine Arts," pp. 982–1089.

119. On Laplace's unusual use of this phrase, see Eric Temple Bell, *Men of Mathematics* (New York: Simon and Schuster, 1961), pp. 176–77, and Morris Kline, *Mathematics: The Loss of Certainty* (New York: Oxford University Press, 1980), p. 62.

120. Owen, *Hysteria, Hypnosis and Healing*.

121. Franz J. Ingelfinger, "Arrogance," *New England Journal of Medicine* 303 (1980): 1507–11.

122. Isaac Asimov, "The Dynamics of an Asteroid," in Harrison, ed., *Beyond Baker Street*, pp. 13–18.

123. Thomas Szasz, *Ceremonial Chemistry: The Ritual Persecution of Drugs, Addicts, and Pushers* (Garden City, N.Y.: Anchor Press, 1974), pp. 83–85.

124. Jean Cocteau, "The Knights of the Round Table," trans. W. H. Auden in *The Infernal Machine and Other Plays*, p. 208.

125. Domenico Comparetti, *Vergil in the Middle Ages* (London: George Allen and Unwin, 1966).

126. M. W. Wellman and W. Wellman, *Sherlock Holmes's War of the Worlds* (New York: Warner, 1975).

127. Arthur Whitaker, "The Case of the Man Who Was Wanted," in *Sherlock Holmes: The Published Apocrypha*, ed. Jack Tracy (Boston: Houghton Mifflin, 1980), p. 306.

128. Charles Dickens, *The Posthumous Papers of the Pickwick Club* (New York: Dodd, Mead & Co., 1944).

129. Lipot Szondi, *Experimental Diagnostics of Drives*, trans. Gertrude Aull (New York: Grune & Stratton, 1952). See also A. T. W. Simeons, *Man's Presumptuous Brain: An Evolutionary Interpretation of Psychosomatic Disease* (New York: E. P. Dutton & Co., 1962), pp. 252–53.

130. Aristotle, *The Nichomachean Ethics*, trans. H. Rackham (Cambridge: Harvard University Press, 1962), pp. 453, 461, 487.

131. T. S. Eliot, *The Complete Poems and Plays 1909–1950* (New York: Harcourt Brace and World, Inc., 1962), p. 125.

132. Samuel Rosenberg, *Naked Is the Best Disguise: The Death and Resurrection of Sherlock Holmes* (Indianapolis, Ind.: Bobbs-Merrill, 1974). See also Maud Bodkin, *Archetypal Patterns in Poetry: Psychological Studies of Imagination* (New York: Vintage, 1958), pp. 102, 238–39.

133. Rudolph Fiehler, *The Strange History of Sir John Oldcastle* (New York: The American Press, 1965); H. S. Bennett, "Sir John Fastolf," *Six Medieval Men and Women* (New York: Atheneum, 1962), pp. 30–68; W. G. Boswell-Stone, *Shakespeare's Holinshed: The Chronicle and the History Plays Compared* (New York: Benjamin Bloom, 1966); the chronicles of Enguerrand de Monstrelet are translated in Peter E. Thompson, *Contemporary Chronicles of the Hundred Years War* (London: Folio Society, 1966).

134. Arthur Waley, trans., *Monkey* (New York: Grove Press, 1958). A complete translation is now available in Anthony C. Yu, *The Journey to the West*, 4 vol. (Chicago: University of Chicago Press, 1977–83).

135. James Goldman, *They Might Be Giants* (New York: Lancer Books, 1970), p. 149.
136. Ibid., pp. 23, 36.
137. Ibid., pp. 25, 37.
138. Ibid., p. 39.
139. Ibid., p. 50.
140. Ibid., p. 29.
141. Ibid., p. 22.
142. Ibid., p. 70.
143. Ibid., p. 44.
144. Paul Engelmann, *Letters From Ludwig Wittgenstein with a Memoir* (New York: Horizon, 1968).
145. Aristotle, *Rhetoric*, book 1, 9 (1367b), trans. W. Rhys Roberts, in *Rhetoric and Poetics* (New York: Modern Library, 1954), p. 61.
146. The use of various readability formulas is discussed in Appendix A of Pasquale Accardo, *A Neurodevelopmental Perspective on Specific Learning Disabilities, Monographs in Developmental Pediatrics* (Baltimore: University Park Press, 1980), 3:189–192.

Bibliography

Auden, W. H. "The Fallen City: Some Reflections on Shakespeare's *Henry IV*." *Encounter*, November 1959.

Baring-Gould, William S. *The Annotated Sherlock Holmes*. 2 vols. New York: Clarkson N. Potter, 1967.

Barthes, Roland. *The Eiffel Tower and Other Mythologies*. New York: Hill and Wang, 1979.

Barzun, Jacques, and Wendell Hertig Taylor. *A Catalogue of Crime*. New York: Harper and Row, 1971.

Beaman, Bruce R. *The Sherlock Holmes Book of Quotations*. Bloomington, Ind.: Gaslight Publications, 1980.

Bosk, C. L. "Occupational Rituals in Patient Management." *New England Journal of Medicine* 303 (1980): 71–76.

Boyd, I. *The Novels of G. K. Chesterton: A Study in Art and Propaganda*. New York: Barnes & Noble, 1975.

Canovan, M. *G. K. Chesterton: Radical Populist*. New York: Harcourt, Brace, Jovanovich, 1977.

Charlesworth, W. R. "The Role of Surprise in Cognitive Development." In *Studies in Cognitive Development: Essays in Honor of Jean Piaget*, edited by D. Elkind and J. H. Flavell, pp. 257–314. New York: Oxford University Press, 1969.

DeWaal, Ronald Burt. *The World Bibliography of Sherlock Holmes and Dr. Watson*. New York: Bramhall House, 1974.

Doyle, Adrian Conan. *A Treasure of Sherlock Holmes*. Garden City, N.Y.: Hanover House, 1955.

Eames, Hugh. *Sleuths, Inc*. Philadelphia: J. B. Lippincott, 1978.

Fabricant, Noah D. "Sherlock Holmes as an Eye, Ear, Nose and Throat Diagnostician." *The Eye, Ear, Nose and Throat Monthly* 36 (1957): 523–26.

Guthrie, Douglas. "Sherlock Holmes and Medicine." *Canadian M.A.J.* 85 (1961): 996–1000.

Hadamard, Jacques. *An Essay on the Psychology of Invention in the Mathematical Field*. New York: Dover, 1954.

Haining, Peter, ed. *A Sherlock Holmes Compendium*. Secaucus, N.J.: Castle Books, 1980.

Hall, Trevor H. *Sherlock Holmes and His Creator*. New York: St. Martin's Press, 1977.

Hardwick, Michael and Millie. *The Sherlock Holmes Companion*. New York: Bramhall House, 1962.

Heath, Peter. *The Philosopher's Alice*. New York: St. Martin's Press, 1974.

Hoyt, Edwin P. *The Improper Bostonian: Dr. Oliver Wendell Holmes*. New York: William Morrow and Company, 1979.

Huxley, Thomas Henry. *On a Piece of Chalk*. New York: Charles Scribner's Sons, 1967.

Lambert, Gavin. *The Dangerous Edge*. New York: Grossman, 1976.

Le Shan, Lawrence. *The Medium, the Mystic and the Physicist: Toward a General Theory of the Paranormal*. New York: Viking, 1974.

Maslow, Abraham H. *The Psychology of Science: A Reconnaissance*. New York: Harper & Row, 1966.

Maull, N. "The Practical Science of Medicine." *Journal of Medicine and Philosophy* 6 (1981): 165–82.

Menke, W. G. "Professional Values in Medicine." *New England Journal of Medicine* 280 (1969): 930–36.

Merton, Robert K. "Singletons and Multiples in Scientific Discovery." *Proceedings of the American Philosophical Society* 105 (1961): 470–86.

Munson, R. "Why Medicine Cannot Be a Science." *Journal of Medicine and Philosophy* 6 (1981): 183–208.

Pearsall, Ronald. *Conan Doyle: A Biographical Solution*. New York: St. Martin's Press, 1977.

Scarlett, E. P. "The Doctor in Detective Fiction." *Archives of Internal Medicine* 118 (1966): 180–86.

Small, Miriam Rossiter. *Oliver Wendell Holmes*. New Haven, Conn.: College and University Press, 1962.

Sperling, Otto. "Appersonation and Eccentricity." *International Journal of Psychoanalysis* 18 (1937).

Stevens, Wallace. *The Palm at the End of the Mind*. New York: Vintage, 1972.

Tracy, Jack. *The Encyclopaedia Sherlockiana or, A Universal Dictionary of the State of Knowledge of Sherlock Holmes and His Biographer John H. Watson, M.D.* New York: Avon Books, 1979.

Wallace, I. *The Fabulous Originals*. New York: Knopf, 1955.

Weimer, W. B. *Notes on the Methodology of Scientific Research*. Hillsdale, N.J.: Lawrence Erlbaum Associates, 1979.

White, P. J. "Medical Leonardo of Boston, Oliver Wendell Holmes, M.D. (1809–1894): An Evaluation of Versatility." *Perspectives in Biology and Medicine* 24 (1981): 411–22.

Wintle, J., and R. Kenin, eds. *Dictionary of Biographical Quotation*. New York: Alfred A. Knopf, 1978.

Wisse, Ruth R. *The Schlemiel as Modern Hero*. Chicago: University of Chicago Press, 1971.

Wood, James Playstead. *The Man Who Hated Sherlock Holmes*. New York: Pantheon, 1965.

Whitehead, Alfred North. *Adventures of Ideas*. New York: Mentor, 1955.

Zweig, Paul. *The Adventurer: The Fate of Adventure in the Western World*. New York: Basic Books, 1974.

Index

Abduction, 66
Accidents, 46, 65
Adler, Irene, 59
Alice (in Wonderland), 95–96
Amis, Kingsley, 67, 125 n.7
Amleth, 61–64
Appearances, 59, 96
Aristotle, 39, 73, 75, 98–100, 111
Arrogance, 18, 90–92, 103, 110
Art, 50, 69, 82, 88–89, 108–10
Arthur, King, 19, 82
Astronomy, 85, 86, 94
Auden, W. H., 101, 103
Austin, James, 66–67

Bacon, Francis, 70–72, 92, 130 n.95
Barthes, Roland, 14–15
Baudelaire, Charles, 88
Beekeeping, 20, 85, 88, 103
Bell, Joseph, 22, 24, 25–30, 33
Bibliophily, 30, 44, 50, 59, 60, 79
Birth: of the hero, 18, 84, 85
Brahe, Tycho, 71
Bruce, Nigel, 99
Brunton, Lauder, 33
Bureaucracy, 21, 25, 45, 78, 104–5
Burton, Richard, 60–61

Cadaver, 13, 31, 62
Carroll, Lewis, 60, 94–97
Catholicism, 25, 107
Cervantes Saavedra, Miguel de, 25, 55, 58, 60, 103, 111
Charcot, Jean-Martin, 29, 90
Chelm, 32–35
Chemistry, 30, 80, 85

Chesterton, G. K., 79–83, 95
Child, 66, 76, 90, 114
Circumstantial evidence, 46, 74
Cocaine, 79, 94
Cocteau, Jean, 68, 94, 129 n.72
Continuations, 23, 50, 60, 82, 110
Creativity, 66, 73, 92–93
Criminology, 80–81, 85, 88
Cryptography, 43, 44, 85

Dandy, 88–89
Dante, 18, 56, 59, 91, 101
D'Artagnan, 51–55, 68
Darwin, Charles, 71–73, 75
Death: of the hero, 20, 82, 85–86
Decentration, 107
De Laplace, Pierre-Simon, 73, 89
De Quincey, Thomas, 89, 108
Derleth, August, 75, 113, 119–21
Dickens, Charles, 23, 25, 98, 100, 101
Disguise, 49, 65, 85, 89
Dodgson, Charles Lutwidge, 92, 94–96
Don Quixote, 50, 55, 57–60, 103, 111
Dostoyevsky, Fyodor, 24, 25
Doyle, Adrian Conan, 22, 24, 101–2
Dreams, 19, 29, 41, 111
Dryden, John, 17, 42, 93
Dumas, Alexandre, 52, 55, 93
Dupin, C. Auguste, 43–49, 93

Einstein, Albert, 75, 106
Eliot, T. S., 101
Empedocles, 85
Ennui, 25, 82
Epic, 17–18
Error, 29, 32–41, 46–47

Facts, 14, 31–32, 39, 56, 70–74, 75, 80
Falstaff, John, 101–3, 104
Father, failed, 32, 58, 127 n.43
Fool, 34–35, 61–64, 77, 101–4, 107–8
Framing sequence, 15, 39, 91–92, 108
Freud, Sigmund, 58, 92, 96, 101, 104–5
Fulgentius, 68

Gaboriau, Emile, 49–50
Galen, 76–77, 127 n.45
Gardner, John, 51, 70
Gardner, Martin, 25, 130 n.93
Gargantua, 19, 41
Genealogy, 63–64, 84–85, 129 n.66
Genetic fallacy, 84–85, 131 n.113
Genius, 78, 92–94, 105
Gerard, Etienne, 23, 126 n.17
Gillette, William, 88, 97
Goldman, James, 57, 70, 104–5, 124

Halsted, William Stewart, 94
Hamlet (character), 60–61, 64, 93, 100, 128 n.64
Henry II (character), 19, 70
Henry V (character), 102–3
Heraclitus, 64, 94
Hero, 18, 50, 51, 89
Hippocrates, 39, 88, 92
Hobbit, 96, 111
Holmes, Abiel, 32, 127 n.43
Holmes, Edwin, 86
Holmes, Gordon, 89, 90
Holmes, Mycroft, 86, 104
Holmes, Oliver Wendell, 23, 30–32, 79, 97
Holmes, Oliver Wendell, Jr., 30
Holmes, Robert, 17
House calls, 109
Hudson, Mrs., 60, 96
Hunting, 50, 66, 68–69
Huxley, T. H., 23, 76

Identity, 89, 96, 103, 104, 106–8
Incest, 61–62, 68, 93

Jung, C. G., 15, 94, 99
Justice, 49, 58, 99–100, 103, 107–8

Kepler, Johannes, 71
Knox, Ronald, 83, 85
Küng, Hans, 70–74, 77–79

Lane, William Arbuthnot, 24, 27
Lecoq, M., 49–50
Locke, John, 38, 57
Louis XIV (character), 52–55
Luck, 66–67

Magic, 26, 29, 59, 89–90, 94
Magnifying lens, 30, 58, 90
Malpractice, 95
Mann, Thomas, 17, 22
Medical education, 13, 26, 29–30, 31, 109
Mill, John Stuart, 66, 73–74, 78
Mind reading, 24, 27, 29, 31, 43, 44, 51, 59, 104
Monkey (character), 104
Moriarity, Professor, 20, 45, 59, 85, 92–94, 104
Munro, Grant, 39–41
Music, 24, 29, 30, 35–36, 85
Myth, 18–21, 32, 70–74, 85–86

Napoleon, 20–21, 27
Newspapers, 24, 43, 47–48
Nicolson, Marjorie, 130 n.88
Nostalgia, 17–18

Occupational medicine, 27–29, 34, 35–38, 85, 126 n.26
Oedipus, 41, 68, 93
Omniscience, 43, 55, 74, 91, 98
Originology, 84–85, 131 n.113
Ortega y Gasset, José, 6, 68–69, 86
Osler, William, 13, 26, 32, 38–39, 47–48, 59, 108

Paget, Sidney, 88
Patricide, 19, 93
Peirce, Charles Saunders, 66
Perdix, 68
Peregrinaggio, 65, 93
Pickwick, Samuel, 98, 100
Pipe, 30, 44, 58
Plato, 59, 86, 92, 93, 111
Plumbism, 37–38
Poe, Edgar Allan, 25, 42–49, 68, 84, 93
Poincaré, Henri, 75–76
Police, 38, 41, 45, 50, 58, 59, 78–81, 93
Popper, Karl, 21
Probability, 38
Profession, 50, 58, 86–88

Index

Proust, Marcel, 96, 101
Psychology, criminal, 46, 51

Quackery, 20, 31, 33–34, 127 n.45

Rabelais, François, 127 n.43
Rathbone, Basil, 81
Regicide, 61, 65, 93
Resurrection, 19, 82
Retroduction, 66
Rhetoric, 90, 112, 125–26 n.14
Richard I (king of England), 19, 20, 125 n.7

Sancho Panza, 58–60, 99, 104
Saxo Grammaticus, 61–64
Sayers, Dorothy, 45, 46, 56, 128 n.52
Science, 13, 21, 31–32, 69, 71–74, 80–81
Serendipity, 64–67
Shakespeare, William, 25, 60, 61, 66, 72, 100, 102–3
Shaw, George Bernard, 22, 24, 68, 71, 97
Sigerson, 85, 131 n.114
Sophrosyne, 91
Sources, fictitious, 19, 60, 65
Spencer, Herbert, 71
Sphinx, 68
Spider's web, 79, 94
Spiritualism, 24, 25, 82
Stevens, Wallace, 17, 32, 33, 42, 50, 51, 57, 85, 92

Sydenham, Thomas, 57
Szondi, Lipot, 99

Theatricality, 20, 31, 45, 85, 89
Time, mythic, 19–21, 85–86, 96
Tobacco, 24, 38, 44, 49, 85, 90
Tracking, 27, 28, 49, 51, 52–55, 56, 65, 74, 128 n.57, 129 n.66
Tramezzino, Michele, 65, 93
Transduction, 66

Unamuno, Miguel de, 60

Victorian age, 15, 18–19, 21, 27, 82, 100, 111
Vidocq, François Eugène, 50–51
Virgil, 18, 94
Voltaire, 56–57, 64, 93

Wallace, Alfred Russel, 25, 72, 73
Walpole, Horace, 65–66
Watsonian deficiencies, 18, 100–101
Weller, Sam, 89, 97–98, 104
Wellman, Manly W., 96, 122
Wells, H. G., 21, 73
Wilson, Jabez, 107–8
Wittgenstein, Ludwig, 70, 75, 96, 105
Woman, 19, 59, 61, 96, 104–5

Zadig, 56–57, 64, 65, 68